LATIN Primer Book III

TEACHER'S EDITION

SECOND EDITION

Martha Wilson

Canon Press

MOSCOW, IDAHO

Martha Wilson, *Latin Primer: Book III (Teacher's Edition), Second Edition*

© 1997 by Martha Wilson
Published 1997 by Canon Press, P.O. Box 8741, Moscow, ID 83843

Printed in the United States of America

ISBN: 1-885767-33-1

TABLE OF CONTENTS

TEACHING NOTES 5

WORD LISTS

WORD LIST 1 13
WORD LIST 2 14
WORD LIST 3 15
WORD LIST 4 16
WORD LIST 5 17
WORD LIST 6 18
WORD LIST 7 19
WORD LIST 8 20
WORD LIST 9 21
WORD LIST 10 22
WORD LIST 11 23
WORD LIST 12 24
WORD LIST 13 25
WORD LIST 14 26
WORD LIST 15 27
WORD LIST 16 28

LESSONS

LESSON 1 31
LESSON 2 33
LESSON 3 36
LESSON 4 38
LESSON 5 39
LESSON 6 42
LESSON 7 44
LESSON 8 47
LESSON 9 49

CROSSWORD PUZZLE 51
CLUES–DOWN 52
CLUES–ACROSS 53

LESSON 10 54

LESSON 11 56
LESSON 12 58
LESSON 13 60
LESSON 14 62
LESSON 15 64
LESSON 16 66
LESSON 17 68
LESSON 18 70
LESSON 19 72
LESSON 20 74
LESSON 21 76
LESSON 22 78
LESSON 23 80
LESSON 24 82
LESSON 25 85
LESSON 26 87
LESSON 27 89
LESSON 28 91
LESSON 29 94
LESSON 30 96
LESSON 31 98
LESSON 32 100
LESSON 33 102
LESSON 34 104
LESSON 35 106
LESSON 36 108
LESSON 37 110
LESSON 38 112
LESSON 39 114
LESSON 40 116
LESSON 41 118
LESSON 42 120
LESSON 43 122
LESSON 44 124
LESSON 45 127
LESSON 46 129
LESSON 47 131
LESSON 48 133

LESSON 49 134
LESSON 50 136
LESSON 51 138
LESSON 52 140
LESSON 53 142
LESSON 54 144
LESSON 55 146
LESSON 56 148
LESSON 57 150
LESSON 58 152
LESSON 59 154
LESSON 60 156
LESSON 61 158
LESSON 62 160
LESSON 63 162
LESSON 64 164
LESSON 65 166
LESSON 66 168
LESSON 67 170
LESSON 68 173
LESSON 69 175
LESSON 70 177
LESSON 71 178
LESSON 72 180
LESSON 73 181
LESSON 74 183

CARMEN POSSUM 187

CHANT SUMMARIES

VERBS 193
NOUNS 193
DEMONSTRATIVES 194
PERSONAL PRONOUNS 194
RELATIVE PRONOUNS 194

TRANSLATIONS

UNIT 4 197
UNIT 5 199
UNIT 6 201
UNIT 7 203
UNIT 8 205
UNIT 9 207
UNIT 10 209

TEST BLANKS

TEST 1 213
TEST 2 215
TEST 3 217
TEST 4 219
TEST 5 221
TEST 6 223
TEST 7 225
TEST 8 227
TEST 9 229
FINAL TEST 230

TEST KEYS

TEST 1 235
TEST 2 237
TEST 3 239
TEST 4 241
TEST 5 243
TEST 6 245
TEST 7 247
TEST 8 249
TEST 9 251
FINAL TEST 252

TEACHING NOTES

UNIT 1 (LESSONS 1-8; WORD LISTS 1 & 2)

Vocabulary review
Review characteristics of Latin nouns, verbs, and adjectives
Review definition of English and Latin nouns, verbs, and adjectives
Translation of present, future, and imperfect tenses

LESSON 4

An example of macaronic verse, "Possum Carmen", is included in the student book. You might want to save it for later.

UNIT 2 (LESSONS 9-14; WORD LISTS 3 & 4)

1st, 2nd, and 3rd declensions
Nominative case for a subject
Accusative case for a direct object
Nominative case for a predicate nominative

UNIT 3 (LESSONS 15-22; WORD LISTS 5 & 6)

Review definition of adjective
Gender
Adjectives matching nouns in gender, number, and case

LESSON 20

The new chant (es, es, ei...) is the pattern for the fifth and last declension.

UNIT 4 (LESSONS 23-30; WORD LISTS 7 & 8)

Verbs
principal parts
use of "ne"
commands
sum, esse, fui, futurum

LESSON 23

It is probably enough for now for the children to be able to call the 1st principal part the present indicative and the 2nd part the infinitive, but it would be good for them to know that there are other infinitives and indicatives.

LESSON 28

Notice that *hic* and *ille*, along with their related forms, are in a different chant format than the rest of the chants in this book. The reason the chants for those words are done that way is because of tradition: they are traditionally learned that way because of the similarity of the endings in the different cases. *Ille* (its many forms included) is a pronoun and adjective meaning "that".

TRANSLATIONS

Translations are given at the back of the book, and are marked according to unit, beginning with Unit 4. They may be used for games, drills, or other extra practice. These are not included in the student book.

UNIT 5 (LESSONS 31-37; WORD LISTS 9 & 10)

Dative case for indirect object
mastery of verb synopsis
introduction of "i" stems:is,is and es,is

LESSON 33

B) In the first example, "wife" is the object of the preposition "to". In the second example, "wife" is an indirect object. But both English sentences are translated into Latin in the same way: by using the dative case for "wife" with no preposition. This is an early example of a distinction in one language that doesn't exist in the other. Just because two things are handled the same in one language doesn't ensure that they will be in the other.

LESSON 34

A neuter noun of the 3rd declension takes the regular characteristics of neuter nouns: The nominative and accusative forms are the same and the nominative and accusative plural ending is "a." They just take these characteristics in the context of the 3rd declension instead of the 2nd where neuter nouns have been encountered before.

An "i" stem merely has an "i" before the "um" in the genitive plural.

UNIT 6 (LESSONS 38-44; WORD LISTS 11 & 12)

Adverbs
Conjunctions: sed, et, -que

LESSON 39

A) A reminder: the stem of *pulcher* is shown to be *pulchr- from its feminine form.*

LESSON 41

#20 on List #12 is left blank for each student to choose from a Latin dictionary their own word that interests them. The supplement for this lesson that is included is an example of what might be done for A) in Lesson 41.

UNIT 7 (LESSONS 45-52; WORD LIST 13)

Genitive of possession
Predicate adjectives

UNIT 8 (LESSONS 53-60; WORD LIST 14)

Perfect tense
Prepositions: per, in, trans

There are three tenses built on the perfect stem: the perfect tense, the pluperfect tense, and the future perfect tense. The perfect tense has been compared to the imperfect tense as a snapshot to a moving picture. The pluperfect has the sense of being before something in the past(I had stood). The future perfect has the sense of being in the past at some future time(I will have stood.)

LESSON 57

"Quintilius Varus, Give back my legions." The verb is in the imperative mood, Quintili Vari is in the vocative case.

UNIT 9 (LESSONS 61-68; WORD LISTS 15 & 16)

Ablative of place in which
3rd-declension "i" stems: neuters ending in e, al, ar
3rd conjugation
Ablative of time when

LESSON 64

You may not want to ask your students to handle a new conjugation this late in the year. If not, make these adjustments:

Skip: Lesson 64
   Lesson 65 B) and C)
   Lesson 66 the last 2 sentences of B), C)
   Lesson 67 the third column of A),
         for B) Use these sentences as replacements.
         1. Agricola animalia in stabulum portavit.
   Lesson 68 A)
         B) the second and fourth sentences

Even without vowel markings, you can tell a 2nd-conjugation verb from one in the 3rd conjugation since the first principal part in the 2nd conjugation ends in "eo," while the first principal part in the 3rd conjugation ends in just "o."

If the children have trouble with the present and future tenses of the 3rd conjugation , this mnenomic device might help: i, o, u are the ending vowels in the present tense, and the remaining vowels, a and e are used in the future tense.

LESSON 66

The ablative of time when or within which does not tell the duration of time. The accusative case is used for that.

UNIT 10 (LESSONS 69-74)

> Grammar and vocabulary review
> Hic, haec, hoc

If you are foregoing the 3rd conjugation for now, make these changes in the unit.

LESSON 70

> A) 7. Potestne portare vir marmorem?
>   8. Adulescens marmorem paene portavit.

LESSON 71

> C) 2. Mensa firma potest portare onus magnum.

LESSON 74

> B) 4. Skip
>   5. Skip

WORD LISTS

WORD LIST 1

1. fenestra, ae	window
2. vultus, ūs	face, expression
3. collum, ī	neck
4. carrus, ī	a two-wheeled wagon
5. rota, ae	wheel
6. dens, dentis	tooth
7. cinis, cineris	ashes, death, destruction
8. nervus, ī	string, sinew
9. ōs, ōris	mouth
10. audācia, ae	boldness
11. culpa, ae	fault, blame, sin
12. rīdeō, rīdēre	laugh, smile
13.* tardō, tardare	slow down, delay
14. aeger, aegra, aegrum	sick, feeble
15. trepidus, a, um	trembling, very frightened

* Bolded numerals indicate vocabulary introduced in previous primers. New vocabulary numerals are not bolded.

Word List 2

1. palma, ae	palm
2. digitus, ī	finger, inch
3. campus, ī	plain, athletic field, level area
4. serpens, serpentis	snake
5. capillus, ī	hair
6. fluvius, ī	river
7. cuspis, cuspidis	point (of a spear)
8. mola, ae	millstone
9. hērōs, herōis	hero
10. argentum, ī	silver, money
11. poena, ae	penalty, punishment
12. portō, portāre	carry
13. lūceō, lūcēre	shine, be bright
14. horrendus, a, um	dreadful, awful, fearful
15. ūmidus, a, um	wet, damp, moist
16. pollex, pollicis	thumb
17. anulus, ī	ring
18. patella, ae	small pan or dish
19. cervix, cervicis	neck (and shoulders)
20. index, indicis	an informer, a sign, the forefinger

WORD LIST 3

1. aurum, ī	gold
2. avāritia, ae	greed
3. humus, ī	ground, earth, land
4. fūmus, ī	smoke
5. incola, ae	inhabitant, settler, colonist
6. laurus, ī	laurel tree
7. regiō, regiōnis	region, direction, area
8. prōvincia, ae	province
9. astrum, ī	star, constellation
10. ventus, ī	wind
11. oppidum, ī	town
12. praemium, ī	reward, prize
13. pecūnia, ae	money
14. cibus, ī	food
15. vīta, ae	life

WORD LIST 4

1. agitō, agitāre   drive, arouse, disturb

2. candeō, candēre   glow, be white

3. convocō, convocāre   call together

4. ardeō, ardēre   burn, blaze

5. ratis, ratis   raft, boat

6. fulmen, fulminis   thunderbolt, lightning

7. lapis, lapidis   stone, rock

8. lūcus, ī   grove

9. sonō, sonāre   resound, sound, roar

10. fons, fontis   spring, fountain, source

11. coma, ae   hair, leaves of a tree, foliage

12. flōs, flōris   flower

13. dēlectō, dēlectāre   delight

14. terreō, terrēre   frighten

15. explōrō, explōrāre   explore

16. mons, montis   mountain

17. silva, ae   forest

18. harēna, ae   sand, beach

19. tempestās, tempestātis   weather, storm

20. equus, ī   horse

Word List 5

1. quiētus, a, um	quiet, at rest, peaceful
2. raucus, a, um	roaring, hoarse
3. citus, a, um	fast, swift
4. densus, a, um	thick, dense
5. dēfessus, a , um	tired, weary
6. perītus, a, um	skilled, experienced
7. epulae, ārum	feast
8. frūmentum, ī	grain, (pl.) crops
9. famulus, ī	male servant
10. famula, ae	female servant
11. caterva, ae	mob, throng
12. locus, ī	place
13. aedificium, ī	building
14. dominus, ī	master, lord
15. via, ae	road, way
16. hortus, ī	garden
17. parō	prepare
18. vītō	avoid
19. torreō	burn, parch, dry up
20. dēmonstrō	show, point out

Word List 6

1. bonus, a, um   good
2. malus, a, um   bad or evil
3. longus, a, um   long
4. fīdus, a, um   faithful, trustworthy
5. novus, a, um   new
6. pūblicus, a, um   public
7. acūtus, a, um   sharp, pointed, intelligent
8. ferus, a, um   fierce
9. gelidus, a, um   cold, like ice
10. laetus, a, um   happy, joyful, glad
11. flamma, ae (f.)   flame
12. custōs, custōdis (m.)   guard, watchman
13. coniunx, coniugis (m. or f.)   husband or wife
14. mercātor, mercātōris (m.)   trader, salesman, merchant
15. grex, gregis (m.)   herd, flock of sheep

WORD LIST 7

1. amō, amāre, amavī, amatum — love
2. clamō, clamāre, clamavī, clamatum — shout
3. hiemō, hiemāre, hiemavī, hiematum — spend the winter
4. laudō, laudāre, laudavī, laudatum — praise
5. navigō, nāvigāre, nāvigavī, nāvigatum — sail
6. mutō, mūtāre, mūtavī, mūtatum — change
7. portō, portāre, portavī, portatum — carry
8. appropinquō (1) — approach, draw near
9. rogō (1) — ask
10. spectō (1) — look at, watch
11. sum, esse, fuī, futūrum — be
12. socius, ī (m.) — ally, companion, associate
13. explōrātor, explōrātōris (m.) — scout, guide, explorer
14. dux, ducis (m.) — leader, guide, general
15. comes, comitis (m.) — companion, fellow-traveler
16. victor, victōris (m.) — victor, winner
17. virgō, virginis (f.) — maiden, young woman
18. labor, labōris (f.) — work, toil, hardship
19. proelium, ī (n.) — battle
20. littera, ae (f.) — letter of the alphabet
    litterae, ārum (f.) — letter (correspondence)

Word List 8

1. peccō, peccāre, peccavī, peccatum	sin
2. iūrō, iūrāre, iūravī, iūratum	swear, conspire, take an oath
3. damnō (1)	condemn
4. conciliō (1)	win, win over
5. conservō (1)	save, preserve
6. reus, ī (m.)	defendant
7. testimōnium, ī (n.)	testimony
8. dēlictum, ī (n.)	wrong, sin, transgression
9. auctōritās, auctōritātis (f.)	authority, influence
10. argūmentum, ī (n.)	proof, evidence
11. iūdex, iudicis (m.)	judge, juror
12. sententia, ae (f.)	opinion, decision
13. latrō, latrōnis (m.)	gangster, robber, highwayman
14. sevērus, a, um	severe, strict, rigid
15. ignārus, a, um	ignorant

Word List 9

1. dō, dare, dedī, datum   give
2. narrō, narrāre, narravī, narratum   tell, relate, recount
3. significō (1)   indicate, point out
4. dēclārō (1)   declare, make clear
5. recitō (1)   recite, read out loud
6. fāma, ae (f.)   rumor, report
7. fābula, ae (f.)   story, legend
8. turba, ae (f.)   crowd, mob, throng
9. benevolentia, ae (f.)   favor, good will
10. populus, ī (m.)   people
11. dōnum, i (n.)   gift
12. vīnum, i (n.)   wine
13. laus, laudis (f.)   praise
14. lex, legis (f.)   law
15. adulēscēns, adulēscēntis (m.)   young man
16. hospes, hospitis (m.)   guest, host
17. mulier, mulieris (f.)   woman
18. iūstus, a, um   just, right, fair, impartial
19. grātus, a, um   grateful, pleasing
20. hodiē   today

WORD LIST 10

1. doceō, docēre, docuī, doctum — teach

2. circumdō, circumdare, circumdedī, circumdatum — put something (acc.) around something (dat.)

3. cantō, cantāre, cantavī, cantatum — sing, play, predict

4. agricola, ae (m.) — farmer

5. cōpia, ae (f.) — supply, (pl.) troops

6. misericordia, ae (f.) — pity, mercy

7. lūdus, ī (m.) — game, play, school

8. bracchium, bracchīi (n.) — arm

9. gaudium, gaudīi (n.) — joy, happiness

10. līberī, ōrum (m.) — children

11. carmen, carminis (n.) — song, chant, poem, prophecy

12. bōs, bovis (m. or f.) — cow, bull, ox, (pl.) cattle

13. māter, matris (f.) — mother

14. pater, patris (m.) — father

15. saepes, saepis (f.) — hedge, fence

16. vallēs, vallis (f.) — valley, vale

17. vestis, vestis (f.) — clothing, garment

18. auris, auris (f.) — ear

19. cārus, a, um — dear, beloved

20. crās — tomorrow

Word List 11

1. cīvis, civis (m.)	citizen
2. praedō, praedōnis (m.)	pirate
3. nāvis, nāvis (f.)	ship
4. avis, avis (f.)	bird
5. carcer, carceris (m.)	prison
6. classis, classis (f.)	fleet (of ships)
7. canis, canis (m. or f.)	dog
8. lītus, lītoris (n.)	shore, shoreline
9. insula, ae (f.)	island
10. fātum, ī (n.)	fate
11. exemplum, ī (n.)	example
12. perīculum, ī (n.)	danger
13. servō, servāre, servavī, servatum	save
14. nuntiō, nuntiāre (1)	announce
15. placeō, placēre, placuī, placitūm	please (be pleasing to)
16. praeclārus, a um	brilliant, clear
17. firmus, a, um	firm, steadfast
18. pulcher, pulchra, pulchrum	beautiful, handsome
19. salvus, a, um	safe, secure, protected
20. bene	well

Word List 12

1. culmen, culminis (n.)	top, peak, high point
2. arbor, arboris (f.)	tree
3. gurges, gurgitis (m.)	whirlpool, eddy, gulf
4. collis, collis (m.)	hill
5. palūs, palūdis (f.)	swamp, bog
6. grāmen, graminis (n.)	grass, greenery
7. iter, itineris (n.)	journey, road, route, trek
8. angustiae, ārum (f.)	narrows, narrow pass, difficulties
9. mēta, ae (f.)	turning point, goal, limit
10. scopulus, ī (m.)	cliff, crag, rock formation
11. antrum, ī (n.)	cave
12. mandō, mandāre, mandavī, mandatum	entrust
13. -que	and (enclitic)
14. sed	but
15. et	and
16. obscūrus, a, um	hidden, dark
17. longinquus, a, um	far away, distant
18. arduus, a, um	steep, lofty
19. celsus, a, um	lofty, high

WORD LIST 13

1. famēs, famis (f.) — hunger, famine, starvation

2. pastor, pastōris (m.) — shepherd

3. imber, imbris (m.) — rain, rainstorm

4. ovis, ovis (f.) — sheep

5. leō, leōnis (m) — lion

6. virtūs, virtūtis (f.) — manliness, courage, strength

7. mors, mortis (f.) — death

8. tenebrae, tenebrārum (f.) — darkness, gloomy place, shadows

9. vestīgium, vestīgī (n.) — footprint, trace, track

10. latebra, ae (f.) — hiding place, lair, hideout

11. constantia, ae (f.) — constancy, steadfastness

12. dīvitiae, ārum (f.) — riches, wealth

13. vulnerō, vulnerāre, vulneravī, vulneratum — wound

14. vexō, vexāre, vexavī, vexatum — harass, vex, ravage, annoy

15. urgeō, urgēre, ursī — urge, press hard

16. impendeō, impendēre, impendī, impensum — threaten, hang over

17. heri — yesterday

18. albus, a, um — white

19. niger, nigra, nigrum — dark, black

20. asper, aspera, asperum — rough, harsh

WORD LIST 14

1. accusō, accusāre, accusavī, accusatum   accuse, blame

2. oppugnō, oppugnāre, oppugnavī,   attack
   oppugnatum

3. postulō, postulāre, postulavī,   demand
   postulatum

4. errō, errāre, erravī, erratum   wander, err, be mistaken

5. stō, stāre, stetī, statum   stand

6. urbs, urbis (f.)   city

7. turris, turris (f.)   tower, turret

8. tectum, ī (n.)   roof, building, dwelling

9. legiō, legiōnis (f.)   legion

10. līmen, līminis (n.)   threshold, doorway

11. per   through

12. in   into

13. trans   across

14. parvus, a, um   small, unimportant

15. prīmus, a, um   first, foremost

Word List 15

1. compleō, complēre, complēvī,   fill, fill up
   complētum

2. caleō, calēre, caluī, calitum   be hot, be warm, glow

3. iaceō, iacēre, iacuī   lie (flat)

4. lacus, lacūs (m.)   lake, hollow

5. secūris, secūris (f.)   axe, hatchet

6. lignum, ī (n.)   wood, timber, firewood

7. marmor, marmoris (n.)   marble

8. iuvenis, iuvenis (m. or f.)   young person

9. senex, senis (m.)   old man

10. nepōs, nepōtis (m.)   grandson, descendant

11. mare, maris (n.)   sea

12. animal, animalis (n.)   animal

13. vallum, ī (n.)   rampart, wall

14. tumulus, ī (m.)   mound, hill, burial mound

15. paene   almost

Word List 16

1. vocō, vocāre, vocāvī, vocatum   call, summon, invite

2. videō, vidēre, vidī, visum   see

3. mittō, mittere, mīsī, missum   send

4. ducō, ducere, duxī, ductum   lead, guide

5. frangō, frangere, frēgī, fractum   break, smash, shatter

6. vincō, vincere, vicī, victum   defeat, conquer

7. emō, emere, ēmī, emptum   buy

8. onus, oneris (n.)   burden, load, weight

9. prīma lucē   at dawn (abl. of time when)

10. vesper, vesperis (m.)   evening, evening star

11. nox, noctis (f.)   night

12. tempus, temporis (n.)   time

13. diēs, diēī (m. and f.)   day, period of time

14. fax, facis (f.)   torch, firebrand

15. simul   (adv.) at the same time

LESSONS

Lesson 1

A) Fill in the blanks about parts of speech.

A noun names a _person_ , _place_ , or _thing_ .

A verb expresses _action_ or _state of being_ .

An adjective describes a _noun_ or a pronoun.

B) Label these words from this week's list according to whether they are nouns (n), verbs (v), or adjectives (a).

1. (n)   cinis/ashes

2. (n)   culpa/fault

3. (a)   trepidus/trembling

4. (n)   fenestra/window

5. (n)   audacia/boldness

6. (n)   vultus/face

7. (v)   rideo/I laugh

8. (n)   collum/neck

9. (a)   aeger/sick

10. (v)   tardo/I delay

C) Translate these sentences.

1. Puella ridet. <u>The girl is laughing.</u>

2. Puella aegra ridebat. <u>The sick girl was laughing.</u>

3. Saxa in via puellam tardabunt. <u>Rocks in the road will delay the girl.</u>

D) Complete from memory the verb chants that are begun below.

amo	amamus	video	videmus	duco	ducimus
amas	amatis	vides	videtis	ducis	ducitis
amat	amant	videt	vident	ducit	ducunt

audio	audimus	sum	sumus	possum	possumus
audis	auditis	es	estis	potes	potestis
audit	audiunt	est	sunt	potest	possunt

LESSON 2

A) COMPLETE EACH STATEMENT ACCORDING TO WHETHER IT IS TRUE OF NOUNS, VERBS, OR ADJECTIVES.

1. <u>Nouns</u> name a person, place, or thing.

2. <u>Adjectives</u> describe a noun or a pronoun. They can tell what kind, which one, how many.

3. <u>Verbs</u> express action or state of being.

4. *a, ae, ae, am* and *a* are endings for <u>nouns</u>.

5. *o, s, t, mus, tis,* and *nt* are endings for <u>verbs</u>.

6. The endings on Latin <u>verbs</u> tell the person and tense.

7. The ending on a Latin <u>noun</u> tells whether it is singular or plural and what its function in the sentence is.

8. Most Latin <u>adjectives</u> have three endings so that they can match the noun they are describing.

9. In a Latin dictionary, a <u>noun</u> is given in its nominative form and its genitive form is also given.

10. In a Latin dictionary, the infinitive is given for a <u>verb</u>.

B) WRITE THE TRANSLATIONS FOR THESE WORDS IN THE FIRST BLANK AND THEIR PLURAL FORMS IN THE SECOND. WHAT PART OF SPEECH ARE THEY ALL? (NOUNS)

1. luna	<u>moon</u>	<u>lunae</u>
2. corona	<u>crown</u>	<u>coronae</u>
3. cibus	<u>food</u>	<u>cibi</u>

4. terra	land or earth	terrae
5. liber	book	libri
6. lupus	wolf	lupi
7. audacia	boldness	audaciae
8. gladius	sword	gladii or gladi

C) PISCIS IS A WORD YOU LEARNED IN THE FIRST BOOK WHICH MEANS FISH. THERE IS A NICE COLLECTION OF LATIN WORDS RELATED TO PISCIS :

piscator, piscatorius, piscatus, pisciculus, piscina, piscinarius, piscor, and piscosus.

You can tell whether they are nouns, verbs, or adjectives by how they are listed in a Latin dictionary. By using a dictionary, write each word, its definition, and the other information that you have learned about it on a line in the correct group. You will probably not recognize the verb from its Latin forms because it is a kind of verb that you have not learned about yet, but look for an English meaning that shows action. *Piscis* is done as an example.

NOUNS

1. piscis, is	a fish
2. piscator, oris	a fisherman
3. piscatus, us	fishes, a catch
4. pisciculus, i	a little fish
5. piscina, ae	a fish-pond
6. piscinarius, i	one fond of fish ponds

VERBS

    1. piscor, ari   to fish

ADJECTIVES

    1. piscatorius, a, um   of fishermen or fishing

    2. piscosus, a, um   abounding in fish

LESSON 3

The etymology of the word *car* is given as follows in a dictionary:

> Middle English *car(re)*, cart, wagon, from Norman French, from Vulgar Latin *carra* (unattested), variant of Latin *carrus*, two-wheeled wagon.

This can be explained using sentences.

> The word *car* came from the Middle English word *car* or *carre* which meant cart or wagon. That came from Norman French which almost certainly came from the Vulgar Latin word *carra*. That was a slightly different spelling of the Latin *carrus*.

Here is the etymology of *ridiculous*:

> Latin *ridiculosus*, laughable, from *ridere*, to laugh.

Write that information in sentences. (Note that if a word is mentioned and its language is not given, you can assume it is the last language mentioned.)

> <u>The English word *ridiculous* came from the Latin word *ridiculosus*, which means "laughable." That came from *ridere*, meaning "to laugh."</u>

Record an etymology on these lines:

_____

_____

and write about it on these:

_____

_____

_____

_____

The French word for *tooth* is *dent* and the Spanish is *diente*. Why are these so similar to the Latin word for *tooth*?

<u>Both French and Spanish are Romance languages, meaning that they came from Latin, the language of the Romans. Therefore, many of the words are similar.</u>

LESSON 4

Macaronic verse or prose is writing that combines two or more languages. These lines are for you to write a macaronic story with English and Latin words, using vocabulary from Word Lists 1 and 2 as well as other Latin words you already know. Try to put Latin subjects, direct objects, and predicate nominatives in their correct case.

LESSON 5

A) FILL IN THE BLANKS.

<u>Verbs</u> express action or state of being.

The verbs from Word Lists 1 and 2 are: (write the infinitive form)

<u>ridere</u>   <u>tardare</u>   <u>portare</u>   <u>lucere</u>

<u>Tardare</u> and <u>portare</u> are in the 1st or "a" conjugation.

<u>Ridere</u> and <u>lucere</u> are in the 2nd or "e" conjugation.

Circle the stems in the verbs you have written above.

The ending of a 1st conjugation is <u>are</u>.

The ending of a 2nd conjugation verb is <u>ere</u>.

B) ON THE LINES BELOW, WRITE THE ENDINGS FOR THE PRESENT, FUTURE, AND IMPERFECT TENSES.

PRESENT		FUTURE		IMPERFECT	
o	<u>mus</u>	bo	<u>bimus</u>	bam	<u>bamus</u>
s	<u>tis</u>	<u>bis</u>	<u>bitis</u>	<u>bas</u>	<u>batis</u>
t	<u>nt</u>	<u>bit</u>	<u>bunt</u>	<u>bat</u>	<u>bant</u>

C) TRANSLATE THESE COMPLETE VERBS.

1. ridemus   <u>we are laughing, we laugh, we do laugh</u>

ridebimus   <u>we shall laugh</u>

ridebamus   <u>we were laughing</u>

2. portat	he carries, he is carrying, he does carry
portabat	he was carrying
portabit	he will carry
3. tardo	I delay, I am delaying, I do delay
tardabo	I shall delay
tardabam	I was delaying
4. lucent	they shine
lucebant	they were shining
lucebunt	they will shine
5. amas	you love
amabas	you were loving
amabis	you will love
6. videtis	you (all) see
videbitis	you (all) will see
videbatis	you (all) were seeing

C) PISCICULUS IN LESSON 2 IS AN EXAMPLE OF A DIMINUTIVE, A WORD FORMED BY ADDING *ULUS*, *OLUS*, *CULUS*, *ELLUS*, OR *ILLUS* TO THE END OF A WORD. IT ADDS THE MEANING OF "LITTLE" TO THE WORD. BELOW ARE DIMINUTIVES FORMED FROM WORDS YOU HAVE LEARNED EARLIER. ON THE FIRST LINE SHOW THE WORD AND SUFFIX THAT WERE COMBINED AND ON THE SECOND LINE WRITE THE MEANING. YOU MAY USE A LATIN DICTIONARY FOR THE MEANING

| 1. pisciculus | piscis + culus | a little fish |
| 2. portula | porta + ula | a little gate |

3. libellus   liber + ellus   a little book

4. viculus   vicus + ulus   a little village

5. ventulus   ventus + ulus   a slight wind

6. saxulum   saxum + ulum   a little rock

7. eculeus   equus +   a little horse, colt

8. corpusculum   corpus + culum   a small body

9. gladiolus   gladius + olus   a small sword

10. homunculus   homo + culus   a little man

LESSON 6

A) AN ADJECTIVE DESCRIBES A NOUN OR A PRONOUN.

The adjectives from Word Lists 1 and 2 are :

　　umidus　　　　horrendus　　　　trepidus　　　　aeger

Find the ten adjectives from this list of words you've learned before. List them on the lines and write their English translations. For any that you don't remember, star them and look them up in your Latin dictionary.

aptus	harena	unda	caecus
bonus	verbum	victoria	via
latus	longinquus	pastor	ventus
flumen	tardus	fidus	possum
rex	avarus	lex	Roma
beatus	parvus	equus	et

1.　aptus　　　　　　　　　suitable, fit, ready

2.　caecus　　　　　　　　blind

3.　bonus　　　　　　　　good

4.　latus　　　　　　　　wide, broad

5.　longinquus　　　　　　far away, distant

6.　tardus　　　　　　　　late, slow, delayed

7.　fidus　　　　　　　　faithful

8.　avarus　　　　　　　　greedy

9.　beatus　　　　　　　　blessed, happy

10. parvus　　　　　　　　little

B) LOOK UP THIS WORD IN YOUR LATIN DICTIONARY: *TIMIDUS*

Is it an adjective? _yes_ How can you tell? <u>by the meaning and the three</u> <u>endings</u>.

Timidus comes from a Latin verb that you've already learned. Can you tell which one? <u>Timeo</u>

C) THE TERMS BELOW WERE SUGGESTED IN A MEDICAL JOURNAL TO GIVE SPECIFIC NAMES TO A GROUP OF BODY PARTS. CAN YOU FIGURE OUT WHAT THESE WOULD REFER TO?

porcellus fori <u>big toe</u> or <u>hallux</u>

porcellus domi <u>the second toe</u>

porcellus carnivorous <u>the third toe</u>

porcellus esuriens* (non voratus) <u>the fourth toe</u>

porcellus plorans domum <u>for the fifth toe</u>

Below is the letter as it appeared in the *New England Journal of Medicine*, Vol 324, No. 7.

> *To the Editor*: When referring to the hand, the names digitus pollicis, indicis, medius, annularis, and minimus specify the five fingers. In situations of clinical relevance the use of such names can preclude anatomical ambiguity. These time-tested terms have honored the fingers, but the toes have been labeled only by number, except of course the great toe, or hallux. Is it not time for the medical community to have the toes no longer stand up and merely be counted? I submit for consideration the following nomenclature to refer to the pedal digits: <u>for the hallux, porcellus fori; for the second toe, p. domi; for</u> <u>the third toe, p. carnivorous; for the fourth toe, p. non voratus*; and for the fifth toe, p.</u> <u>plorans domum</u>.
>
> Using *porcellus* as the diminutive form of *porcus*, one can translate the suggested terminology as follows: piglet at market, piglet at home, meat-eating piglet, piglet having not eaten, and piglet crying homeward, respectively.
>
> John Phillips
>
> Yale University School of Medicine

Esuriens replaces *non voratus* in the children's work, but it has the same meaning as that intended—"hungering piglet."

LESSON 7

A) TRANSLATE THESE INTO LATIN VERBS.

1. They are laughing.   <u>rident</u>

2. She will see.   <u>videbit</u>

3. It is bright.   <u>lucet</u>

4. They will delay.   <u>tardabunt</u>

5. We are carrying.   <u>portamus</u>

6. You will smile.   <u>ridebis</u>

B) UNDERLINE THE CORRECT LATIN TRANSLATION.

1. *The farmer is carrying the wheel.*

   Agricola rota portat.
   Agricolam rota portabit.
   <u>Agricola rotam portat.</u>

2. *The wild animal is showing (its) teeth.*

   Ferum dentem demonstrat.
   <u>Ferus dentes demonstrat.</u>
   Ferus dentos demonstrat.

3. *The stream will delay the chariot.*

   Fluvium carrus tardabit.
   <u>Carrum fluvius tardabit.</u>
   Carros fluvius tardabunt.

C) Fill in the blanks.

A noun that is used as a subject is put in the nominative case.

A noun that is used as a direct object is put in the accusative case.

D) Both Latin and Greek are much used in medicine. Choose some of the words below and record their medical meanings. All of these words are derivatives of words on your first two lists.

patella   the kneecap

nerve   any of the bundles of fibers interconnecting the central
                 nervous system and the organs or parts of the body.

bicuspid   a tooth having two points

molar   a tooth with a broad crown for grinding food

capillary   one of the minute blood vessels that connect the
                 arteries and the veins

The fingers already have Latin names that doctors use: digitus pollicis, d. annularis, d. minimus, d. indicis, and d. medius. By translating these terms, label correctly the fingers of the hand below.

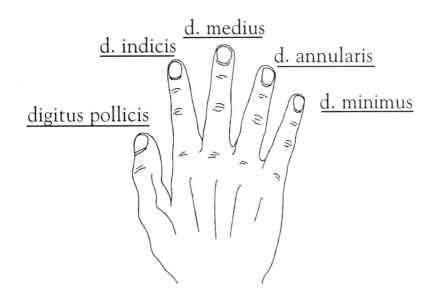

E) COMPLETE THESE CHANTS.

o	mus	bo	bimus	bam	bamus
s	tis	bis	bitis	bas	batis
t	nt	bit	bunt	bat	bant

i	imus	ero	erimus	eram	eramus
isti	istis	eris	eritis	eras	eratis
it	erunt	erit	erint	erat	erant

r	mur	bor	bimur	bar	bamur
ris	mini	beris	bimini	baris	bamini
tur	ntur	bitur	buntur	batur	bantur

LESSON 8

A) Underline the nouns, circle the verbs, and translate these sentences.

1. <u>Fluvius</u> (lucet)   <u>The river is shining.</u>

2. <u>Heros</u> (ridet)   <u>The hero laughs.</u>

3. <u>Carri</u> (tardabunt)   <u>The chariots will delay.</u>

4. <u>Poena</u> (est) horrenda.   <u>The punishment is dreadful.</u>

B) Circle the endings of these verbs, translate them and write "p" if they are present tense, "f" if they are future tense, and "i" if they are imperfect tense.

1. ride(bit)   <u>he, she, or it will laugh</u>   <u>f</u>

2. luce(t)   <u>he, she, or it is bright</u>   <u>p</u>

3. ama(tis)   <u>you (all) do love</u>   <u>p</u>

4. porta(nt)   <u>they are carrying</u>   <u>p</u>

5. porta(bam)   <u>I was carrying</u>   <u>i</u>

6. vide(bimus)   <u>we shall see</u>   <u>f</u>

7. tarda(batis)   <u>you all were delaying</u>   <u>i</u>

What two things do verb endings tell you?   <u>the person and the tense</u>

C) Guess at the meaning of these words and then look up them up and write the meaning.

1. audacious	fearlessly daring, bold
2. incinerate	to consume by burning, to burn or burn up
3. culpable	responsible for wrong or error, blameworthy
4. defenestration	the act of throwing someone or something out of a window
5. intrepid	fearless, bold
6. trepidation	a state of alarm or dread; a trembling

D) Write the complete etymologies of derivatives of three words from Word Lists 1 and 2 on these lines.

_____

_____

_____

_____

_____

_____

E) What do you think the Spanish word *culpa* and the Italian word *colpa* both mean? GUILT, BLAME, FAULT

LESSON 9

A) *Incola* is an interesting word when compared with *agricola*, *monticola*, *silvicola*, and *caelicola*. Look up each of these in your Latin dictionary and write their definitions next to them.

1. agricola   <u>farmer</u>

2. monticola   <u>a highlander</u>

3. silvicola   <u>inhabiting woods</u>

4. caelicola   <u>dwelling in heaven</u>

What do they all have in common in their meaning? (You will probably have to think more about *agricola* to fit it in with the rest.)

     <u>They all have to do with inhabiting someplace</u>.

What do they all have in common in their spelling?   <u>icola</u>

B) The chemical symbol for gold comes from its name in Latin. This is also true for a few other of the elements. By using the English-to-Latin section of your Latin dictionary, match the chemical symbols on the left with the elements on the right. The first one is done for you.

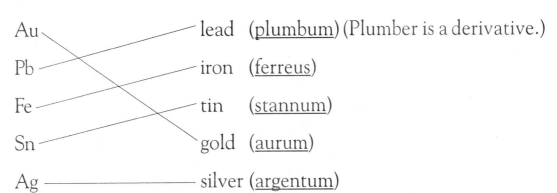

Au — lead (<u>plumbum</u>) (Plumber is a derivative.)

Pb — iron (<u>ferreus</u>)

Fe — tin (<u>stannum</u>)

Sn — gold (<u>aurum</u>)

Ag ———————— silver (<u>argentum</u>)

The Latin name for mercury is *argentum vivum.* Can you translate that? <u>living silver; (or "quick silver" using the old meaning of "quick" as "living," as in the Apostles' Creed: "to judge the quick and the dead")</u>.

C) List one or two derivatives for each of these words.

1. provincia   <u>provincial</u>   <u>province</u>

2. vita   <u>vital</u>   <u>vitamin</u>   <u>vitality</u>

3. ventus   <u>vent</u>   <u>ventilate</u>

D) What is the word for "star" that you have learned before? <u>STELLA</u> <u>Terra</u> is the word for "land or earth" that you already know.

E) Compare these words for *gold* in three Romance languages.

Spanish	French	Italian
oro	*or*	*oro*

F) Complete these chants of noun endings.

a	<u>ae</u>	us	<u>i</u>	um	<u>a</u>
<u>ae</u>	<u>arum</u>	<u>i</u>	<u>orum</u>	<u>i</u>	<u>orum</u>
<u>ae</u>	<u>is</u>	<u>o</u>	<u>is</u>	<u>o</u>	<u>is</u>
<u>am</u>	<u>as</u>	<u>um</u>	<u>os</u>	<u>um</u>	<u>a</u>
<u>a</u>	<u>is</u>	<u>o</u>	<u>is</u>	<u>o</u>	<u>is</u>

x	<u>es</u>	is	<u>es</u>	us	<u>us</u>
<u>is</u>	<u>um</u>	<u>is</u>	<u>ium</u>	us	<u>uum</u>
<u>i</u>	<u>ibus</u>	<u>i</u>	<u>ibus</u>	<u>ui</u>	<u>ibus</u>
<u>em</u>	<u>es</u>	<u>em</u>	<u>es</u>	<u>um</u>	<u>us</u>
<u>e</u>	<u>ibus</u>	<u>e</u>	<u>ibus</u>	<u>u</u>	<u>ibus</u>

CROSSWORD PUZZLE

ON THE NEXT TWO PAGES YOU WILL FIND THE CLUES FOR FILLING THE BLANKS OF THIS CROSSWORD PUZZLE. FOLLOW CLOSELY THE INSTRUCTIONS GIVEN WITH THE CLUES.

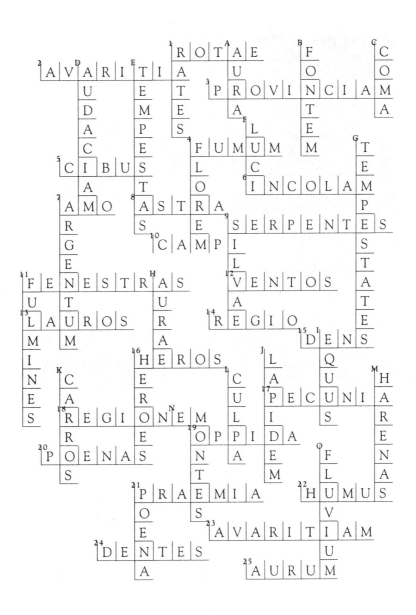

CROSSWORD CLUES–DOWN

TRANSLATE THE UNDERLINED WORD INTO LATIN. YOU WILL NEED TO PAY ATTENTION TO ITS FUNCTION IN THE SENTENCE (I.E.,* WHETHER IT IS A SUBJECT, DIRECT OBJECT, OR PREDICATE NOMINATIVE).

1. They watched the <u>boats</u> from the bluff.
4. Jack picked the <u>flower</u>.
7. The <u>silver</u> was very shiny.
9. <u>Forests</u> covered all the islands.
11. <u>Thunderbolts</u> lit the entire valley.
16. The <u>heroes</u> returned from the war.
21. A spanking was the <u>punishment</u>.
A. The <u>breeze</u> shook the yellow leaves from the trees.
B. They could see the <u>spring</u> between the rocks.
C. The <u>foliage</u> was red.
D. The captain noticed the <u>boldness</u> of the boy.
E. The <u>storm</u> came suddenly.
F. <u>Groves</u> of aspen grew on the hillsides.
G. They remembered few <u>storms</u> as harsh as this.
H. <u>Breezes</u> blew all day long.
I. The <u>horse</u> sat down.
J. The jeweler admired the <u>stone</u>.
K. A long wall stopped the <u>chariots</u>.
L. The <u>sin</u> was great.
M. The sailors saw the <u>beaches</u> of the island at dawn.
N. Cloudy <u>mountains</u> stood beyond the fields.
O. Two deer crossed the <u>river</u> at dusk.

*i.e. is an abbreviation of two Latin words: *id est*, which means, "that is." This abbreviation is often found in English writing.

CROSSWORD CLUES—ACROSS

ACCORDING TO ITS DECLENSION, PUT EACH WORD IN THE CASE AND NUMBER GIVEN. YOU WILL NEED TO TRANSLATE THE WORDS IN ITALICS INTO LATIN. THE OTHERS ARE ALREADY IN LATIN.

1. rota in nominative plural
2. *greed* in nominative singular
3. provincia in accusative singular
4. *smoke* in accusative singular
5. *food* in nominative singular
6. incola in acc. sing.
7. *I love*
8. *constellation* nom. pl.
9. serpens in nom. pl.
10. campus in nom. pl.
11. *window* in acc. pl.
12. *wind* in acc. pl.
13. laurus in acc. pl.
14. *region* in nom. sing.
15. *tooth* in nom. sing.
16. *hero* in nom. sing.
17. *money* in nom. sing.
18. *region* in acc. sing.
19. oppidum in nom. pl.
20. poena in acc. pl.
21. *reward* in acc. pl.
22. *ground, earth, land* in nom. sing.
23. avaritia in acc. sing.
24. dens in acc. pl.
25. *gold* in nom. sing.

What was the only verb in that list?   <u>amo</u>

LESSON 10

A) DECLINE THESE NOUNS ON THE LINES, LABEL THE CASES TO THE LEFT, AND WRITE THE ENDINGS TO THE RIGHT.

NOM.	laurus	lauri	us	i
GEN.	lauri	laurorum	i	orum
DAT.	lauro	lauris	o	is
ACC.	laurum	lauros	um	os
ABL.	lauro	lauris	o	is

NOM.	incola	incolae	a	ae
GEN.	incolae	incolarum	ae	arum
DAT.	incolae	incolis	ae	is
ACC.	incolam	incolas	am	as
ABL.	incola	incolis	a	is

NOM.	regio	regiones	x	es
GEN.	regionis	regionum	is	um
DAT.	regioni	regionibus	i	ibus
ACC.	regionem	regiones	em	es
ABL.	regione	regionibus	e	ibus

NOM.	astrum	astra	um	a
GEN.	astri	astrorum	i	orum
DAT.	astro	astris	o	is
ACC.	astrum	astra	um	a
ABL.	astro	astris	o	is

B) As the prescription is read, write the corresponding ending on the line.

1. 1st dec. nom. pl. <u>ae</u>
2. 1st dec. acc. sing. <u>am</u>
3. 2nd dec. acc. sing. <u>um</u>
4. 3rd dec. nom. pl. <u>es</u>
5. 2nd dec. nom. pl. <u>i</u>

6. 2nd dec. acc. pl. <u>os</u>
7. 2nd dec. neut. nom. pl. <u>a</u>
8. 2nd dec. neut. acc. pl. <u>a</u>
9. 1st dec. acc. pl. <u>as</u>
10. 3rd. dec. acc. sing. <u>em</u>

C) Give the nominative and accusative forms for these words in Latin.

	NOMINATIVE	ACCUSATIVE
1. provinces	<u>provinciae</u>	<u>provincias</u>
2. towns	<u>oppida</u>	<u>oppida</u>
3. regions	<u>regiones</u>	<u>regiones</u>
4. gold	<u>aurum</u>	<u>aurum</u>
5. laurel trees	<u>lauri</u>	<u>lauros</u>

LESSON 11

A) LIST THE NOUNS FROM THIS WEEK'S WORDS.

1. ratis

2. fulmen

3. lapis

4. lucus

5. fons

6. coma

7. flos

8. mons

9. silva

10. harena

11. tempestas

12. equus

B) CHOOSE ONE WORD FROM THE 1ST DECLENSION AND ONE WORD FROM THE 2ND DECLENSION TO DECLINE IN THE APPROPRIATE BOXES. (THE WORD FOR THE 3RD DECLENSION HAS ALREADY BEEN CHOSEN FOR YOU.) TO THE RIGHT OF EACH BOX, LIST THE REST OF THE NOUNS FROM THE LIST IN THAT DECLENSION.

1ST DECLENSION

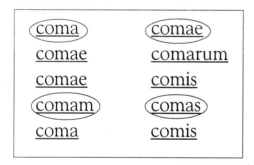

coma	comae
comae	comarum
comae	comis
comam	comas
coma	comis

(harena)
(coma)
(silva)

2ND DECLENSION

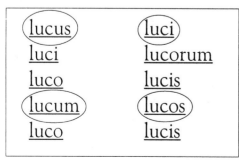

lucus	luci
luci	lucorum
luco	lucis
lucum	lucos
luco	lucis

(equus)

3RD DECLENSION

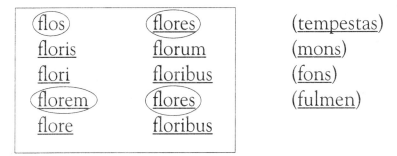

flos   flores   (tempestas)
floris   florum   (mons)
flori   floribus   (fons)
florem   flores   (fulmen)
flore   floribus

Circle the nominative and accusative forms (singular and plural) in each declension.

C) WHAT DO ALL OF THESE WORDS MEAN?   FLOWER

Spanish	French	Italian
flor	*fleur*	*fiore*

LESSON 12

A) IN THE PARENTHESES, WRITE THE TRANSLATIONS FOR THESE NOUNS. THEN GIVE THE ACCUSATIVE SINGULAR FORM FOR EACH ACCORDING TO ITS DECLENSION. PAY ATTENTION TO STEMS.

1. harena   (sand, beach   )   harenam

2. lucus   (grove   )   lucum

3. fons   (spring, fountain   )   fontem

4. mons   (mountain   )   montem

5. tempestas   (weather, storm   )   tempestatem

6. lapis   (stone, rock   )   lapidem

7. silva   (forest   )   silvam

8. incola   (inhabitant, settler)   incolam

In the 1st declension the accusative ending is <u>am</u>. In the 2nd declension it is <u>um</u>. In the 3rd it is <u>em</u>.

B) TRANSLATE THESE SENTENCES ACCORDING TO THE CASES USED FOR THE NOUNS.

1. Incola montem explorat. <u>The settler is exploring the mountain.</u>

2. Harenam incola videbit. <u>The settler will see the beach.</u>

3. Incolam tempestas terret. <u>The storm frightens the colonist.</u>

4. Equus lapidem portabit. <u>A horse will carry the rock.</u>

5. Incolam fons delectat. <u>The spring delights the settler.</u>

6. Fulmen candet. <u>The lightning glows.</u>

C) Use the vocabulary from Word Lists 3 and 4 to determine the definition of these English words.

1. An *incandescent* light bulb

      a) is large   b) <u>glows with heat</u>   c) is expensive

2. A *sylvan* place

      a) <u>has woods</u>   b) has fairies   c) is mountainous

3. A *lapidary* inscription is

      a) lengthy   b) <u>engraved on stone</u>   c) inaccurate

4. *Floriculture* is the cultivation of

      a) manners   b) vegetables   c) <u>flowers</u>

5. An *aureate* evening is

      a) <u>golden</u>   b) dark   c) windy

6. *Humus* <u>A brown or black organic substance consisting of decayed vegetable matter that provides nutrients for plants.</u>

D) There is an English word in this lesson whose singular and plural form reflects the declension of a 3rd declension noun. Can you find it? (It is in the plural form.) <u>PARENTHESES</u>

LESSON 13

A) A VERB EXPRESSES <u>ACTION</u> OR <u>STATE</u> <u>OF</u> <u>BEING</u>.

When verbs express being, they do not take direct objects.

On the lines, conjugate *sum* in the present tense. Give the translations next to the forms.

<u>I am</u>	SUM	<u>SUMUS</u>	<u>we are</u>
<u>you are</u>	<u>ES</u>	<u>ESTIS</u>	<u>you (all) are</u>
<u>he, she, it is</u>	<u>EST</u>	<u>SUNT</u>	<u>they are</u>

B) TRANSLATE THESE SENTENCES CONTAINING SOME FORM OF *SUM*.

1. Praemium est pecunia. <u>The reward is money.</u>

2. Insulae sunt montes. <u>The islands are mountains.</u>

3. Nautae sunt incolae. <u>The sailors are settlers.</u>

4. Regio est provincia. <u>The region is a province.</u>

5. Luci erant lauri. <u>The groves were laurel trees.</u>

6. Nauta erit heros. <u>The sailor will be a hero.</u>

The nouns in the sentences above are all in the <u>nominative</u> case. Some of the nouns are subjects and some are <u>predicate nominatives</u>.

C) TRANSLATE THESE SENTENCES CONTAINING DIRECT OBJECTS.

1. Ventus comam agitat. <u>The wind is disturbing the leaves of the tree.</u>

2. Avaritia incolam agitat. <u>Greed drives the settler.</u>

3. Equum tempestas terret. <u>The weather is frightening the horse.</u>

D) Translate these sentences into Latin. Make sure that you put all the nouns in the right case.

1. The region is a forest. <u>Regio est silva.</u>

2. The settlers will explore the region. <u>Incolae regionem explorabunt.</u>

LESSON 14

A) DECLINE *FLOS, COMA,* AND *LUCUS* ON THE LINES.

flos	flores		coma	comae
floris	florum		comae	comarum
flori	floribus		comae	comis
florem	flores		comam	comas
flore	floribus		coma	comis

lucus	luci
luci	lucorum
luco	lucis
lucum	lucos
luco	lucis

B) COMPLETE THESE LATIN SENTENCES BY TRANSLATING THE ENGLISH WORDS IN PARENTHESES INTO THEIR CORRECT FORM IN LATIN. THESE SENTENCES ARE IN ENGLISH ORDER RATHER THAN THEIR USUAL LATIN ORDER. BE READY TO GIVE THE TRANSLATIONS OF THE COMPLETE SENTENCES.

1. Nauta convocabit (the boats). rates–The sailor will call together the boats.

2. Roma est (a town). oppidum–Rome is a town.

3. Aurum delectat (the settlers). incolas–Gold delights the settlers.

4. (The river) tardabit incolas. fluvius (or flumen)–The river will delay the settlers.

5. Tempestas terret (the horse). equum–The storm frightens the horse.

6. Flos (delights) puellam. delectat–The flower delights the girl.

C) ANSWER THESE QUESTIONS ABOUT THE SENTENCES ON THE PREVIOUS PAGE.

In #1, what is the function of *nauta?*   <u>subject</u>

In #2, what is the function of *oppidum?*   <u>predicate nominative</u>

In #3, what is the tense of *delectat?*   <u>present</u>

In #4, what is the tense of *tardabit?*   <u>future</u>

In #5, what is the case of *tempestas?*   <u>nominative</u>

In #6, what is the function of *puellam?*   <u>direct object</u>

LESSON 15

A) COMPLETE THESE DEFINITIONS.

A noun names a person , place , or thing .

A verb expresses action or state of being .

An adjective modifies (or describes) a noun or a pronoun. It can tell which one, what kind, or how many.

B) FILL IN THE BLANKS AND THE BOXES AS DIRECTED.

The masculine form of *citus* is citus . The feminine form is cita and the neuter form is citum .

Decline each in the spaces below according to its declension. (The masculine form is in the 2nd declension, the feminine form is in the 1st declension, and the neuter form, not surprisingly, declines like a neuter noun of the 2nd declension.)

MASCULINE		FEMININE	
citus	citi	cita	citae
citi	citorum	citae	citarum
cito	citis	citae	citis
citum	citos	citam	citas
cito	citis	cita	citis

NEUTER	
citum	cita
citi	citorum
cito	citis
citum	cita
cito	citis

C) COMPARE THESE WORDS FOR *BUILDING* IN THESE FOUR ROMANCE LANGUAGES.

Spanish	Italian	French	Portuguese
edificio	*edificio*	*edifice*	*edificio*

What is the other major Romance language? <u>Romanian</u>

LESSON 16

A) EXAMINE THIS LIST OF NOUNS.

1. caterva, ae (f.)	crowd
2. via, ae (f.)	road
3. fenestra, ae (f.)	window
4. famula, ae (f.)	female servant
5. famulus, i (m.)	male servant
6. locus, i (m.)	place
7. hortus, i (m.)	garden
8. equus, i (m.)	horse
9. ventus, i (m.)	wind
10. oppidum, i (n.)	town

f. stands for FEMININE, m. stands for MASCULINE, and n. stands for NEUTER.

If the list above is typical, most 1st declension nouns are feminine .

Most 2nd declension nouns are masculine . 2nd declension nouns that end in *um* are neuter .

B) TRANSLATE THESE PHRASES INTO LATIN. THE ADJECTIVE NEEDS TO MATCH THE NOUN IN GENDER AND NUMBER.

1. roaring crowd	caterva rauca
2. roaring wind	ventus raucus

3. thick window   <u>fenestra densa</u>

4. swift horse   <u>equus citus</u>

5. swift horses   <u>equi citi</u>

6. skilled male servant   <u>famulus peritus</u>

7. quiet road   <u>via quieta</u>

8. quiet town   <u>oppidum quietum</u>

9. quiet roads   <u>viae quietae</u>

10. quiet towns   <u>oppida quieta</u>

11. weary female servants   <u>famulae defessae</u>

12. dense garden   <u>hortus densus</u>

C) REVIEW THE FIRST TWO CHANTS BY WRITING THEM ON THE LINES AND BEGIN TO LEARN THE NEXT ONE.

is	<u>es</u>	us	<u>us</u>	u	ua
is	<u>ium</u>	us	<u>uum</u>	us	uum
<u>i</u>	<u>ibus</u>	<u>ui</u>	<u>ibus</u>	u	ibus
<u>em</u>	<u>es</u>	<u>um</u>	<u>us</u>	u	ua
<u>e</u>	<u>ibus</u>	<u>u</u>	<u>ibus</u>	u	ibus

LESSON 17

A) ALTHOUGH IT IS NOT NECESSARY, A COMMON PLACE FOR AN ADJECTIVE IS AFTER THE NOUN OR PRONOUN THAT IT MODIFIES. THIS IS TRUE OF THE SENTENCES BELOW. TRANSLATE THESE SENTENCES.

1. Equus defessus oppidum vitat. <u>The weary horse avoids the town.</u>

2. Famula perita dominum placet. <u>The skilled servant pleases the master.</u>

3. Flammae et fumus densus viam occultant. <u>The flames and dense smoke hide the way.</u>

4. Incola quietum locum demonstrat. <u>The settler points out the quiet place.</u>

5. Ventus raucus fluvium agitat. <u>The roaring wind disturbs the river.</u>

B) DECLINE THE LATIN TRANSLATION OF *SWIFT HORSE* BELOW.

<u>equus citus</u>	<u>equi citi</u>
<u>equi citi</u>	<u>equorum citorum</u>
<u>equo cito</u>	<u>equis citis</u>
<u>equum citum</u>	<u>equos citos</u>
<u>equo cito</u>	<u>equis citis</u>

C) CONSIDER THESE DERIVATIVES.

Torrid is a derivative of *torreo*. The Torrid Zone is the region of the earth's surface between the tropics of Cancer and Capricorn. Why would that make sense? <u>Because the Torrid Zone is the equatorial region, which is hot, dry, and "burning."</u>

Raucous is a derivative of *raucus*. Look up *raucous* in an English dictionary and write its definition on the line. <u>harsh, stringent; rowdy, disorderly</u>

LESSON 18

A) You have already learned that an adjective needs to match the noun or pronoun that it modifies in gender and number. They also have to match each other in case. Fill in these lists:

GENDER refers to whether a noun is   <u>masculine</u>

or   <u>feminine</u>

or   <u>neuter</u>

NUMBER refers to whether a noun is   <u>singular</u>

or   <u>plural</u>

The five CASES that
you have learned are

<u>nominative</u>
<u>genitive</u>
<u>dative</u>
<u>accusative</u>
<u>ablative</u>

If a noun is masculine, singular, and in the accusative case, the adjective that describes it will have to be <u>masculine</u>, <u>singular</u>, and in the <u>accusative</u> case.

B) Translate the phrase *happy girl* into Latin and then decline it.

<u>puella laeta</u>   <u>puellae laetae</u>
<u>puellae laetae</u>   <u>puellarum laetarum</u>
<u>puellae laetae</u>   <u>puellis laetis</u>
<u>puellam laetam</u>   <u>puellas laetas</u>
<u>puella laeta</u>   <u>puellis laetis</u>

C) GIVE THESE FORMS OF *HAPPY GIRL* IN LATIN.

1. nominative singular   puella laeta

2. accusative singular   puellam laetam

3. nominative plural   puellae laetae

4. accusative plural   puellas laetas

D) ONE WAY THAT A NOUN AND THE ADJECTIVE DESCRIBING IT DO *NOT* NEED TO MATCH IS IN DECLENSION. KEEPING THAT IN MIND, TRANSLATE THESE PHRASES. GIVE EACH IN ITS NOMINATIVE SINGULAR FORM.

1. faithful watchman   custos fidus

2. happy wife   coniunx laeta

3. happy husband   coniunx laetus

4. intelligent merchant   mercator acutus

5. new herd   grex novus

LESSON 19

A) AN ADJECTIVE <u>DESCRIBES</u> A <u>NOUN</u> OR A PRONOUN. IT CAN TELL WHICH ONE, <u>HOW MANY</u>, OR WHAT KIND. IN LATIN, AN ADJECTIVE MUST MATCH THE NOUN OR <u>PRONOUN</u> IT MODIFIES IN <u>GENDER</u>, <u>NUMBER</u>, AND <u>CASE</u>.

B) DECLINE THESE PHRASES ON THE LINES BELOW. BE ESPECIALLY CAREFUL WITH THE LAST ONE.

via publica	<u>viae publicae</u>
<u>viae publicae</u>	<u>viarum publicarum</u>
<u>viae publicae</u>	<u>viis publicis</u>
<u>viam publicam</u>	<u>vias publicas</u>
<u>via publica</u>	<u>viis publicis</u>

TRUSTWORTHY MALE SERVANT

<u>famulus fidus</u>	<u>famuli fidi</u>
<u>famuli fidi</u>	<u>famulorum fidorum</u>
<u>famulo fido</u>	<u>famulis fidis</u>
<u>famulum fidum</u>	<u>famulos fidos</u>
<u>famulo fido</u>	<u>famulis fidis</u>

NEW BUILDING

<u>aedificium novum</u>	aedificia nova
<u>aedificii novi</u>	<u>aedificiorum novorum</u>
<u>aedificio novo</u>	<u>aedificiis novis</u>
<u>aedificium novum</u>	<u>aedificia nova</u>
<u>aedificio novo</u>	<u>aedificiis novis</u>

QUIET HERD

grex quietus   greges quieti
gregis quieti   gregum quietorum
gregi quieto   gregibus quietis
gregem quietum   greges quietos
grege quieto   gregibus quietis

C) TRANSLATE THESE SENTENCES.

1. Grex ventum gelidum vitat. The flock is avoiding the cold wind.

2. Famula fida hortum parabit. The faithful female servant will prepare the garden.

3. Frumentum mercator acutus demonstrat. The intelligent merchant points out the grain.

4. Flames will parch the thick grain. Flammae frumentum densum torrebunt.

LESSON 20

A) THE GENDER OF MOST 1ST DECLENSION NOUNS IS <u>FEMININE</u>.

There are, however, a few nouns in the 1st declension that are masculine. The most common ones are:

poeta, which means	<u>poet</u>
agricola, which means	<u>farmer</u>
incola, which means	<u>settler</u>
nauta, which means	<u>sailor</u>

With the exception of *incola*, which can also be feminine, these are all people who were always men in Roman times.

B) TRANSLATE *EXPERIENCED SAILOR* AND DECLINE IT.

<u>nauta peritus</u>	<u>nautae periti</u>
<u>nautae periti</u>	<u>nautarum peritorum</u>
<u>nautae perito</u>	<u>nautis peritis</u>
<u>nautam peritum</u>	<u>nautas peritos</u>
<u>nauta perito</u>	<u>nautis peritis</u>

C) IN CHOOSING THEIR DEFINITIONS, CONSIDER THE SOURCES OF THESE DERIVATIVES OF WORDS IN WORD LIST 6.

1. Circle the <u>two</u> correct definitions for *acute*.

(not blunt)   pretty   distant   (shrewd)

2. If something is *flammable* it (circle one)

> is difficult to see
>
> is pleasant to cook and eat
>
> (tends to ignite easily and burn rapidly)

(Here is a funny thing about *flammable: inflammable* means the same thing.)

3. *Custody* is

> (the act or right of guarding)
>
> the top of a chimney
>
> a dessert

What is another derivative of *custos*?   <u>custodian</u>

D) This chant will follow *u, us, u, u, u*. After saying it with the class, say it to yourself and practice writing it on the extra lines.

#1		#2		#3	
es	es	___ ___	___ ___	___ ___	___ ___
ei	erum	___ ___	___ ___	___ ___	___ ___
ei	ebus	___ ___	___ ___	___ ___	___ ___
em	es	___ ___	___ ___	___ ___	___ ___
e	ebus	___ ___	___ ___	___ ___	___ ___

LESSON 21

A) WRITE THE NAMES OF THE CASES IN ORDER.

1. <u>nominative</u> (<u>subject</u>)

2. <u>genitive</u>

3. <u>dative</u>

4. <u>accusative</u> (<u>direct object</u>)

5. <u>ablative</u>

Write "subject" next to the case used for that function and "direct object" next to the case used for that.

B) TRANSLATE THESE PHRASES INTO LATIN, MATCHING GENDER, NUMBER, AND CASE.

(NOMINATIVE CASE)

1. public building   <u>aedificium publicum</u>

2. long way   <u>via longa</u>

3. peaceful gardens   <u>horti quieti</u>

4. roaring wind   <u>ventus raucus</u>

5. new buildings   <u>aedificia nova</u>

(ACCUSATIVE CASE)

1. public buildings   <u>aedificia publica</u>

2. long roads   <u>vias longas</u>

3. peaceful garden   <u>hortum quietum</u>

4. roaring winds   <u>ventos raucos</u>

5. new building   <u>aedificium novum</u>

C) TRANSLATE THESE INTO LATIN.

1. The fierce flames burn up the garden. <u>Flammae ferae hortum torrent.</u>

2. The experienced servant will prepare the grain. <u>Famulus peritus frumentum parabit.</u>

3. The flock avoids the roaring crowd. <u>Grex catervam raucam vitat.</u>

EXTRA CREDIT

In Latin prose, an adjective is normally next to the noun it modifies. In poetry it can be quite a different matter. Try these sentences which are like poetry in that respect.

1. Avaritia incolam malum magna agitat. <u>Great greed drives the evil settler.</u>

2. Novus carrus coniugem portat defessam. <u>The new chariot carries the weary wife.</u>

3. This doesn't contain adjectives, but it is the first line from a famous Latin poem.

    Arma virumque cano. <u>Arms and the man I sing. (Virgil's Aeneid)</u>

LESSON 22

A) USE THIS VOCABULARY TO SUPPLEMENT THE VOCABULARY THAT YOU HAVE WORKED WITH THIS YEAR.

1. leo, leonis (m.)	lion
2. praefectus, i (m.)	officer
3. arbor, arboris (f.)	tree
4. sagittarius, i (m.)	archer
5. carcer, carceris (m.)	prison
6. finitimi, orum (m.)	neighbors
7. homo, hominis (m.)	man
8. captivus, i (m.)	captive
9. dux, ducis (m.)	leadser, guide
10. formica, ae (m.)	ant
11. familia, ae (f.)	household
12. lingua, ae (f.)	language

B) TRANSLATE AS MANY OF THESE AS YOU CAN. YOU MAY HAVE TO LOOK UP A FEW WORDS.

1. Dux incolas convocabit. <u>The leader will call together the settlers.</u>

2. Harena longa nautas defessos delectat. <u>The long beach delights the weary sailors.</u>

3. Sagitarii periti locum videbunt. <u>The skillful archers will see the place.</u>

4. Famula fida epulam parat. <u>The faithful (female) servant prepares the feast.</u>

5. Finitimi quieti oppidum malum vitant. <u>The peaceful neighbors avoid the wicked town</u>

6. Leo raucus incolam trepidum terrebat. <u>The roaring lion was frightening the trembling settler.</u>

7. Coniunx bonus Dominum amat. <u>The good husband loves the Lord.</u>

8. Homines montes altos explorabunt. <u>The men will explore the high mountains.</u>

9. Lingua aliena incolas novos perturbat. <u>The foreign language confuses the new settlers.</u>

10. Arbores densae heroem tardat. <u>The dense trees delay the hero.</u>

11. Familia aedificium gelidum vitat. <u>The household avoids the cold building.</u>

12. Captivi miseri carcerem humidum vitabant. <u>The unhappy captives were avoiding the wet prison.</u>

LESSON 23

A) TO BE ABLE TO USE A NOUN IN LATIN, YOU NEED TO KNOW ITS NOMINATIVE AND GENITIVE FORM, ITS GENDER, AND ITS MEANING. FILL IN THESE BLANKS REGARDING THAT INFORMATION.

The <u>nominative</u> form is the form of a word that you use to look it up in the dictionary.

The <u>gender</u> of a noun tells you whether you will need the masculine, feminine, or neuter form of an adjective to modify it.

You can tell the declension of a noun from the <u>genitive</u> form.

You can find out the base of a noun from its <u>genitive</u> form.

The <u>genitive</u> ending is *ae* in the 1st declension, *i* in the 2nd declension, and *is* in the 3rd declension.

B) JUST AS YOU NEED TO MEMORIZE BASIC INFORMATION FOR EACH NOUN, THERE IS BASIC INFORMATION FOR EACH VERB THAT YOU NEED TO LEARN. THE BASIC INFORMATION FOR A VERB IS ITS FOUR PRINCIPAL PARTS.

1. amo, amare, amavi, amatum

2. laudo, laudare, laudavi, laudatum

3. hiemo, hiemare, hiemavi, hiematum

4. clamo, clamare, clamavi, clamatum

5. navigo, navigare, navigavi, navigatum

Examine this example and follow it. Although you need to know the four principal parts of verbs from now on, you only need to be familiar with the names of the first two.

1. *Amo* is the present active indicative. It means " I love."

Amare is the present active infinitive. It means "to love".

2. *Laudo* is the <u>present</u> active indicative. It means <u>I praise</u>.

Laudare is the <u>present</u> active <u>infinitive</u>. It means <u>to praise</u>.

3. <u>*Hiemo* is the present active indicative. It means "I spend the winter."</u>

<u>*Hiemare* is the present active infinitive. It means "to spend the winter."</u>

4. <u>*Clamo, etc.*</u> _____

_____

_____

5. <u>*Navigo, etc.*</u> _____

_____

_____

All of these verbs are in the <u>1st</u> conjugation. You can tell this because their stems all end in <u>a</u> .

LESSON 24

A) HERE ARE THE PRESENT ACTIVE INFINITIVES OF MOST OF THE VERBS FROM THIS WEEK. UNDERLINE THE PART THAT IS THE STEM.

<u>am</u>are   <u>clam</u>are   <u>hiem</u>are   <u>laud</u>are   <u>navig</u>are

<u>mut</u>are   <u>port</u>are   <u>appropinqu</u>are   <u>rog</u>are   <u>spect</u>are

B) THE STEM THAT YOU UNDERLINED IS THE PRESENT STEM AND IS USED FOR THREE TENSES: THE PRESENT, THE FUTURE, AND THE IMPERFECT. CONJUGATE THE PRESENT TENSE OF AMO ON THE LINES AND TRANSLATE IT ON THE SIDES.

<u>I love</u>	AMO	AMAMUS	<u>we love</u>
<u>you love</u>	AMAS	AMATIS	<u>you (all) love</u>
<u>he loves</u>	AMAT	AMANT	<u>they love</u>

What person and number is the only place that the entire present stem is not used in the present tense? <u>1st person singular</u>

Now conjugate and translate AMO in the future tense.

<u>I shall love</u>	AMABO	AMABIMUS	<u>we shall love</u>
<u>you will love</u>	AMABIS	AMABITIS	<u>you (all) will love</u>
<u>he will love</u>	AMABIT	AMABUNT	<u>they will love</u>

C) THE IMPERFECT TENSE ALSO USES THE PRESENT STEM. THE ENDINGS FOR THE IMPERFECT TENSE ARE <u>BAM</u>, <u>BAS</u>, <u>BAT</u>, <u>BAMUS</u>, <u>BATIS</u>, <u>BANT</u>. CONJUGATE AND TRANSLATE AMO IN THIS TENSE BELOW.

<u>I was loving</u>	AMABAM	AMABAMUS	<u>we were loving</u>
<u>you were loving</u>	AMABAS	AMABATIS	<u>you (all) were loving</u>
<u>he was loving</u>	AMABAT	AMABANT	<u>they were loving</u>

D) USING THE CORRECT STEMS AND ENDINGS, GIVE THESE VERB FORMS IN LATIN.

1. I shout	<u>clamo</u>
I shall shout	<u>clamabo</u>
I was shouting	<u>clamabam</u>
2. you are sailing	<u>navigas</u>
you will sail	<u>navigabis</u>
you were sailing	<u>navigabas</u>
3. she is asking	<u>rogat</u>
she will ask	<u>rogabit</u>
she was asking	<u>rogabat</u>
4. we do watch	<u>spectamus</u>
we shall watch	<u>spectabimus</u>
we were watching	<u>spectabamus</u>
5. you (all) praise	<u>laudatis</u>
you (all) will praise	<u>laudabitis</u>
you (all) were praising	<u>laudabatis</u>
6. they are approaching	<u>appropinquant</u>
they will approach	<u>appropinquabunt</u>
they were approaching	<u>appropinquabant</u>

E) SUM WAS NOT INCLUDED IN TODAY'S WORK BECAUSE IT IS IRREGULAR. GIVE ITS FOUR PRINCIPAL PARTS ON THE LINE.

<u>sum</u>   <u>esse</u>   <u>fui</u>   <u>futurum</u>

F) TAKE NOTE OF HOW *APPROPINQUO* IS USED IN THE SENTENCES BELOW.

Dux ad montes appropinquat.
The guide is drawing near to the mountains.

Flammae appropinquabant ad silvam.
Flames were approaching the forest.

Although there are other ways to use *appropinquo,* in this book you will be using *ad* with it when referring to place.

LESSON 25

A) FROM MEMORY, GIVE THE REST OF THE PRINCIPAL PARTS OF THESE VERBS:

CLAMO	clamare	clamavi	clamatum
MUTO	mutare	mutavi	mutatum
PORTO	portare	portavi	portatum
SPECTO	spectare	spectavi	spectatum
SUM	esse	fui	futurum

B) COMPLETE THE CHANTS THAT GIVE THE ENDINGS FOR THESE TENSES:

present:	o	s	t	mus	tis	nt
imperfect:	bam	bas	bat	bamus	batis	bant
future:	bo	bis	bit	bimus	bitis	bunt

C) TRANSLATE THESE VERBS INTO ENGLISH.

1. laudabam   I was praising

2. appropinquat   he is approaching

3. spectabit   she will watch

D) You already know the present, future, and imperfect tenses of *sum*. To refresh your memory, conjugate *sum* on the lines in those tenses and give the translations on the sides. Notice that the future of *sum* is declined differently from the future perfect declension of other verbs (*ero, eris, erit, erimus, eristis, erint*).

PRESENT

I am	SUM	SUMUS	we are
you are	ES	ESTIS	you(all) are
he, she, it is	EST	SUNT	they are

FUTURE

I will be	ERO	ERIMUS	we will be
you will be	ERIS	ERITIS	you(all) will be
he will be	ERIT	ERUNT	they will be

IMPERFECT

I was	ERAM	ERAMUS	we were
you were	ERAS	ERATIS	you(all) were
he was	ERAT	ERANT	they were

E) Give the translation of these sentences.

1. Comites erant. <u>They were fellow-travelers.</u>

2. Victores laeti clamant. <u>The happy victors are shouting.</u>

3. Explorator hiemabit. <u>The scout will spend the winter.</u>

4. Dux fidus appropinquabat. <u>The faithful guide was approaching.</u>

5. Proelium erit longum. <u>The battle will be long.</u>

6. Eramus defessi viri. <u>We were tired men.</u>

LESSON 26

A) A QUICK REVIEW:

What part of speech names a person, place, or thing? <u>noun</u>

If a Latin noun is the subject of a sentence, in what case is it? <u>nominative</u>

If it is a direct object? <u>accusative</u>

If it is a predicate nominative? <u>nominative</u>

B) WRITE THESE SENTENCES IN LATIN, REMEMBERING WHAT YOU HAVE LEARNED ABOUT NOUNS, ADJECTIVES, AND VERBS. A FEW OF THE WORDS ARE ONES YOU HAVEN'T STUDIED THIS YEAR, SO YOU MAY HAVE TO USE YOUR LATIN DICTIONARY IN ORDER TO USE THEM CORRECTLY.

1. The evil robbers were conspiring. <u>Latrones mali iurabant.</u>

2. The general loves the young woman. <u>Dux virginem amat.</u>

3. The new teacher will praise the good student. <u>Magister novus discipulum bonum laudabit.</u>

4. The defendant is a gangster. <u>Reus est latro.</u>

5. The judge was watching the trembling defendant. <u>Iudex reum trepidum spectabat.</u>

C) TRANSLATE THESE SENTENCES, PAYING PARTICULAR ATTENTION TO THE TENSE OF THE VERBS AND THE CASE OF THE NOUNS.

1. Exploratores ad regionem gelidam appropinquant. The explorers are approaching the cold region.

2. Dux proelium ferum spectabat. The general was watching the fierce battle.

3. Fumum ventus portabat. The wind was carrying the smoke.

4. Mercator litteras portabit. The merchant will carry the letter.

LESSON 27

A) CONJUGATE *SUM* ON THE LINES IN THE PRESENT, FUTURE AND IMPERFECT TENSES.

PRESENT		FUTURE		IMPERFECT	
sum	sumus	ero	erimus	eram	eramus
es	estis	eris	eritis	eras	eratis
est	sunt	erit	erunt	erat	erant

Compare this present tense Spanish conjugation of the being verb to the present tense Latin conjugation you did above.

I am	SOY	SOMOS	we are
you are	ERES	SOIS	you (all) are
he is	ES	SON	they are

B) WRITE DOWN THE CHANT THAT BEGINS WITH *EGO* AND ENDS WITH *VOBIS*. SOME OF THE BLANKS ARE FILLED IN FOR YOU.

ego	tu	nos	vos
mei	tui	nostrum	vestrum
mihi	tibi	nobis	vobis
me	te	nos	vos
me	te	nobis	vobis

Nos appears twice in this chant. In the nominative case it means <u>we</u>, and in the accusative case it means <u>us</u>.

C) ITALIAN, FRENCH, PORTUGUESE, ROMANIAN, AND <u>SPANISH</u> ARE CALLED <u>ROMANCE LANGUAGES</u> BECAUSE <u>THEY ALL COME FROM THE LANGUAGE OF THE ROMANS (LATIN)</u>.

Here are the principal parts of the verb meaning "defeat, overcome, conquer":

vinco   vincere   vici   victum

The words below, all meaning "victor," each came from this verb. But they did not all come from the same form. The French word *vainqueur* came from the second principal part, while the English word came from another part. Which one do you think it was? <u>fourth</u>

English	Spanish	Italian	French
victor	*vencedor*	*vincitore*	*vainqueur*

D) In the Spanish Bible, the words below appear in one of the New Testament books. Can you find out what they say? The underlined words are words that you can figure out from the work today or from other Latin that you already know. (The last word is not first person singular as it would be in Latin, but the basic meaning of the verb is what you know.)

<u>somos</u> mas que <u>vincadores</u> por medio de aquel que <u>nos</u> <u>amo</u>

The words "por medio de" are a phrase meaning "by means of" (or "through").

Translation?

<u>We are more than conquerors through him who loves us.</u>

E) Translate these sentences.

1. Silva densa vos occultabit. <u>The dense forest will hide you (all).</u>

2. Serpens magnus nos terret. <u>The big snake is frightening us.</u>

3. Fons gelidus me delectabat. <u>The cold spring was delighting me.</u>

Lesson 28

A) Translate these verbs by giving the correct infinitive form.

1. to shout   clamare
2. to change   mutare
3. to sail   navigare
4. to love   amare
5. to approach   appropinquare
6. to watch   spectare
7. to ask   rogare
8. to spend the winter   hiemare
9. to carry   portare
10. to sin   peccare
11. to swear   iurare
12. to win   conciliare
13. to preserve   conservare
14. to condemn   damnare
15. to praise   laudare
16. to be   esse

Circle the present stem contained in those verbs. (Don't do #16.)

B) Use those stems to form these verbs in Latin. Label each for tense.

1. he will condemn   damnabit   future

2. you are sinning   peccas   present

3. I was approaching   appropinquabam   imperfect

4. they were sailing   navigabant   imperfect

5. we shallchange   mutabimus   future

6. you(all) are shouting   clamatis   present

C) As you learned in the last book, the present stem can be used for commands to one person. Remember, also, to command more than one person, add -te to the stem. Translate these.

1. Ama.   Love.

2. Amate.   (You all) Love.

3. Clamate!   Shout!

4. Specta proelium.   Watch the battle.

5. Portate equum.   (You all) carry the horse.

6. Lauda Deum.   Praise God.

D) Complete this chant that you already know:

hic	haec	hoc	hi	hae	haec
huius	huius	huius	horum	harum	horum
huic	huic	huic	his	his	his
hunc	hanc	hoc	hos	has	haec
hoc	hac	hoc	his	his	his

And here is a new one for you to learn.

ille	illa	illud		illi	illae	illa
illius	illius	illius		illorum	illarum	illorum
illi	illi	illi		illis	illis	illis
illum	illam	illud		illos	illas	illa
illo	illa	illo		illis	illis	illis

LESSON 29

A) TRANSLATE THESE QUESTIONS. MAKE SURE YOU HAVE THE CORRECT TENSE.

1. Iurabitne reus? <u>Will the defendant take an oath?</u>

2. Hiemabantne exploratores? <u>Were the explorers spending the winter?</u>

3. Estne iudex severus? <u>Is the judge severe?</u>

4. Eratne reus honestus? <u>Was the defendant honest?</u>

5. Eritne coniunx laetus? <u>Will the husband be happy?</u>

To form a Latin question, <u>ne</u> is added to the end of the first word in the sentence. The first word in questions is usually the <u>verb</u>.

B) TRANSLATE THESE.

1. The defendant was taking an oath. <u>Reus iurabat.</u>

2. The evidence will save the defendant. <u>Argumentum reum conservabit.</u>

3. The jurors will condemn the gangster. <u>Iudices latronem damnabunt.</u>

4. Testimonium ignarum reum damnat. <u>The ignorant testimony is condemning the defendant.</u>

5. Argumentum iudices conciliabat. <u>The proof was winning over the jurors.</u>

C) BELOW ARE THE PRINCIPAL PARTS OF VERBS THAT YOU HAVE HAD EARLIER THIS YEAR. N.B. *SONO* HAS A THIRD PRINCIPAL PART THAT IS DIFFERENT FROM THE USUAL PATTERN.

1. tardo	tardare	tardavi	tardatum
2. porto	portare	portavi	portatum
3. agito	agitare	agitavi	agitatum
4. convoco	convocare	convocavi	convocatum
5. sono	sonare	sonui	sonatum
6. delecto	delectare	delectavi	delectatum
7. exploro	explorare	exploravi	exploratum
8. paro	parare	paravi	paratum
9. vito	vitare	vitavi	vitatum
10. demonstro	demonstrare	demonstravi	demonstratum

LESSON 30

A) ONE GOOD WAY OF PRACTICING WITH VERBS IS TO DO A SYNOPSIS. HERE IS AN EXAMPLE.

SIN <u>pecco, peccare, peccavi, peccatum</u>

> third person plural

>> *present*   <u>peccant</u>

>> *future*   <u>peccabunt</u>

>> *imperfect* <u>peccabant</u>

The first step is to write the principal parts of the verb that you are working with. The second step is to give the forms for the person and number specified in all the tenses that you know.

Do these synopses in the same way.

CHANGE <u>muto, mutare, mutavi, mutatum</u>

> third person singular

>> *present*   <u>mutat</u>

>> *future*   <u>mutabit</u>

>> *imperfect* <u>mutabat</u>

CONSPIRE <u>iuro, iurare, iuravi, iuratum</u>

> second person plural

>> *present*   <u>iuratis</u>

>> *future*   <u>iurabitis</u>

>> *imperfect* <u>iurabatis</u>

B) Translate these commands and questions into Latin.

1. Avoid sin. (A command to more than one person) Vitate delictum.

2. Save the town. (Singular) Conserva oppidum.

3. Is the judge strict? Estne iudex severus?

4. Was the maiden happy? Eratne virgo laeta?

5. Is the leader watching the battle? Spectatne dux proelium?

LESSON 31

A) DO THE VERB SYNOPSES BY LISTING THE PRINCIPAL PARTS OF EACH VERB AND THE CORRECT FORM IN EACH TENSE.

READ OUT LOUD <u>recito, recitare, recitavi, recitatum</u>

> first person plural
>
>> *present* <u>recitamus</u>
>>
>> *future* <u>recitabimus</u>
>>
>> *imperfect* <u>recitabamus</u>

GIVE <u>do, dare, dedi, datum</u>

> third person singular
>
>> *present* <u>dat</u>
>>
>> *future* <u>dabit</u>
>>
>> *imperfect* <u>dabat</u>

B) COMPLETE THE DECLENSION OF THESE NOUNS.

benevolentia	benevolentiae	populus	populi
benevolentiae	benevolentiarum	populi	populorum
benevolentiae	benevolentiis	populo	populis
benevolentiam	benevolentias	populum	populos
benevolentia	benevolentiis	populo	populis

vinum	vina	lex	leges
vini	vinorum	legis	legum
vino	vinis	legi	legibus
vinum	vina	legem	leges
vino	vinis	lege	legibus

laus	laudes
laudis	laudum
laudi	laudibus
laudem	laudes
laude	laudibus

C) Write the names of the cases in order on the lines.

1. nominative   4. accusative

2. genitive   5. ablative

3. dative

D) Write the dative and accusative forms of these words and then circle the endings.

	DATIVE	ACCUSATIVE
1. benevolentia	benevolentiae	benevolentiam
2. populus	populo	populum
3. vinum	vino	vinum
4. lex	legi	legem
5. laus	laudi	laudem

LESSON 32

The subject of a Latin sentence is put in the <u>nominative</u> *case. A direct object is put in the* <u>accusative</u> *case. Today we will learn a use for the dative case.*

A) LABEL THE SUBJECT AND DIRECT OBJECT IN THESE SENTENCES AND THEN TRANSLATE THEM INTO LATIN.

                 s.   d.o.

1. The woman shows good will. <u>Mulier benevolentiam demonstrat.</u>

                 s.   d.o.

2. The guest tells the rumor. <u>Hospes famam narrat.</u>

B) TRANSLATE THESE SENTENCES INTO ENGLISH. START WITH THE VERB, LOOK FOR THE SUBJECT, THEN FIND A DIRECT OBJECT. TRANSLATE THAT MUCH OF ALL THE SENTENCES, LEAVING ANY WORDS IN THE DATIVE CASE FOR LAST.

1. Mulier vinum hospiti dat. <u>The woman is giving wine to the guest.</u>

2. Rex legem populi dabit. <u>The king will give the law to the people.</u>

3. Mulier benevolentiam hospiti demonstrabat. <u>The woman was showing good will to the guest.</u>

4. Adulescens laudem Deo dabat semper. <u>The young man was always giving praise to God.</u>

5. Nuntius victoriam populi declarat. <u>The messenger is announcing the victory to the people.</u>

6. Adulescens fabulam sorori recitabat. <u>The young man was reading aloud the story to the sister.</u>

Usually the dative case can be translated into English by using "to" or "for." Finish the translation of the sentences above with that in mind.

C) DO A VERB SYNOPSIS OF *NARRO* FOR THE SECOND PERSON SINGULAR.

(PRINCIPAL PARTS) <u>narro, narrare, narravi, narratum</u>

present <u>narras</u>

future <u>narrabis</u>

imperfect <u>narrabas</u>

LESSON 33

A) GIVE THE NOMINATIVE, GENITIVE, AND DATIVE SINGULAR FORMS FOR THESE NOUNS WHICH YOU HAVE LEARNED THIS YEAR.

	NOMINATIVE	GENITIVE	DATIVE
1. window	fenestra	fenestrae	fenestrae
2. laurel tree	laurus	lauri	lauro
3. husband	coniunx	coniugis	coniugi
4. gold	aurum	auri	auro

Write a Latin sentence using at least two of those nouns. One noun in the sentence must be in the dative case. Give the translation of your sentence.

_____

_____

B) CONSIDER THIS LATIN SENTENCE AND THE TWO ENGLISH TRANSLATIONS OF IT.

Vir coniugi flores dabit.   *The man will give flowers to his wife.*
                                    The man will give his wife flowers.

Although the English sentences are different from each other, they mean the same thing, and both are correct translations of the dative case.

C) TRANSLATE THESE SENTENCES. ABOVE THE LATIN NOUNS WRITE THE CASE AND ABOVE THE LATIN VERBS WRITE THE TENSE AND PERSON.

       n.   acc.   dat.   f., 3rd

1. Dominus lucum hospiti monstrabit. <u>The master will point out the grove to the guest.</u>

    n.   acc.   dat.   f., 3rd

2. Rex victoriam populo declarabit hodie. <u>The king will declare the victory to the people today.</u>

    n.   acc.   dat.   p., 3rd

3. Mulier pecuniam adulescenti dat. <u>The woman is giving money to the young man.</u>

    n.   acc.   dat.   p., 3rd

4. Pater donum filio grato dat. <u>The father is giving a gift to the grateful son.</u>

    n.   acc.   dat.   imp., 3rd

5. Pater fabulas filiis quietis recitabat. <u>The father was reading aloud the legends to the quiet sons.</u>

    n.   acc.   dat.   imp., 3rd

6. Femina cenam familiae parabat. <u>The woman was preparing supper for the household.</u>

LESSON 34

A) Decline each of these 3rd declension nouns according to its kind. The first one is a regular 3rd declension noun, the second is a neuter 3rd declension noun, and the third one is an i-stem 3rd declension noun. Remember how neuter nouns and i-stems are declined.

pater	patres	carmen	carmina
patris	patrum	carminis	carminum
patri	patribus	carmini	carminibus
patrem	patres	carmen	carmina
patre	patribus	carmine	carminibus

vestis	vestes
vestis	vestium
vesti	vestibus
vestem	vestes
veste	vestibus

B) Write the dative forms of these nouns.

	SINGULAR	PLURAL
1. famulus	famulo	famulis
2. liberi	******	liberis
3. copia	copiae	copiis
4. mater	matri	matribus
5. pater	patri	patribus

C) PRACTICE USING *CIRCUMDO*.

CIRCUMDO means to put something(acc.) around something(dat.)

1. Vestem adulescenti circumdat. <u>He is putting the garment around the young man.</u>

2. Bracchium matri circumdat. <u>He is putting his arm around the mother.</u>

3. Copias valli circumdat. <u>He is putting troops around the valley.</u>

4. Saepem loco circumdant. <u>They are putting a fence around the place.</u>

D) TRANSLATE THESE SENTENCES.

1. Pater carmen liberis cantabat. <u>The father was singing a song to the children.</u>

2. Latro aurum socio dat. <u>The robber gives the gold to the associate.</u>

3. Agricola boves liberis monstrat. <u>The farmer is showing the cows to the children.</u>

E) DO A SYNOPSIS FOR *CANTO* IN 1ST PERSON PLURAL.

CANTO <u>canto, cantare, cantavi, cantatum</u>

present <u>cantamus</u>

future <u>cantabimus</u>

imperfect <u>cantabamus</u>

LESSON 35

A) DO A SYNOPSIS OF DOCEO IN THE 3RD PERSON SINGULAR.

DOCEO   <u>doceo, docere, docui, doctum</u>

       present   <u>docet</u>

       future   <u>docebit</u>

       imperfect   <u>docebat</u>

DOCEO takes the accusative case for both the thing and the person taught. Practice using it in these translations.

Pater carmina liberos docebit. <u>The father will teach the children songs.</u>

The woman is teaching the little boy the letters. <u>Mulier puerum parvum litteras docet.</u>

B) TRANSLATE THESE SENTENCES.

1. Victor misericordiam copiis demonstrabat. <u>The victor was showing mercy to the troops.</u>

2. Agricola saepem villae circumdabit. <u>The farmer will put a fence around the farmhouse.</u>

3. The happy guest is singing a song for the family. <u>Hospes laetus familiae carmen cantat.</u>

4. The guest will be hoarse tomorrow. <u>Hospes erit raucus cras.</u>

C) YOU WILL BE LEARNING, BEGINNING NOW, HOW TO RECOGNIZE 3RD DECLENSION NOUNS THAT ARE I-STEMS. THERE ARE THREE DIFFERENT GROUPS OF 3RD DECLENSION NOUNS THAT DECLINE IN THIS WAY. THE FIRST GROUP HAS TWO QUALIFICATIONS:

The nominative form ends in -is or -es

and

the genitive and nominative forms have the same number of syllables.

There are four nouns from this week's list that belong to this group. What are they?

1. saepes   2. valles   3. vestis   4. auris

Complete these chants for the 3rd declension, regular and i- stem:

x	es	is	es
is	um	is	ium
i	ibus	i	ibus
em	es	em	es
e	ibus	e	ibus

D) CHOOSE A DERIVATIVE OF A WORD FROM WORD LIST 9 OR 10. WRITE ITS ETYMOLOGY HERE.

_____

_____

_____

LESSON 36

A) GIVE A SYNOPSIS OF *CIRCUMDO* IN THE 2ND PERSON SINGULAR.

CIRCUMDO <u>circumdo, circumdare, circumdedi, circumdatum</u>

> *present* <u>circumdas</u>
>
> *future* <u>circumdabis</u>
>
> *imperfect* <u>circumdabas</u>

B) GIVE THE DATIVE FORMS OF THESE NOUNS AND CIRCLE THEIR ENDINGS.

	SINGULAR	PLURAL
1. saepes	<u>saepi</u>	<u>saepibus</u>
2. misericordia	<u>misericordiae</u>	<u>misericordiis</u>
3. ludus	<u>ludo</u>	<u>ludis</u>
4. bracchium	<u>bracchio</u>	<u>brachiis</u>

C) DECLINE THIS NOUN. IN WHAT DECLENSION IS IT ?　<u>3RD</u>

valles	<u>valles</u>
vallis	<u>vallium</u>
<u>valli</u>	<u>vallibus</u>
<u>vallem</u>	<u>valles</u>
<u>valle</u>	<u>vallibus</u>

Why are "valles," "vestis," "auris," and "saepes" all i-stems? <u>They have the same number of syllables in the nominative and genitive forms, and the nominative form ends in -es or -is.</u>

D) Translate these sentences.

1. Agricola adulescenti benevolentiam monstrabit. <u>The farmer will show good will to the young man.</u>

2. Victores leges populo recitabant. <u>The victors were reading aloud the laws to the people.</u>

3. Mulier vestem hospiti dabat. <u>The woman was giving clothing to the guest.</u>

4. Liberi grati donum patri demonstrant. <u>The grateful children are showing the gift to the father.</u>

5. Agricola saepem bovibus circumdat. <u>The farmer is putting a fence around the cows.</u>

LESSON 37

A) LISTED HERE ARE THE PRINCIPAL PARTS OF THE REST OF THIS YEAR'S VERBS. YOU HAVE NOT LEARNED THESE PRINCIPAL PARTS YET. YOU SHOULD LEARN THEM NOW. FROM MEMORY, WRITE THE DEFINITION OF THESE WORDS IN THE BLANKS.

1. torreo, torrere, torrui, tostum   <u>burn, parch, roast</u>

2. placeo, placere, placui, placitum   <u>please</u>

3. rideo, ridere, risi, risum   <u>laugh</u>

4. luceo, lucere, luxi   <u>shine</u>

5. candeo, candere, candui   <u>glow, be white</u>

6. ardeo, ardere, arsi, arsum   <u>burn, blaze</u>

7. terreo, terrere, terrui, territum   <u>frighten</u>

B) DO A SYNOPSIS OF *RIDEO* IN THE 3RD PERSON PLURAL.

RIDEO <u>rideo, ridere, risi, risum</u>

     present <u>rident</u>

     future <u>ridebunt</u>

     imperfect <u>ridebant</u>

C) NEXT TO THESE ENGLISH DERIVATIVES OF LATIN WORDS FROM WORD LISTS 9 AND 10, WRITE THE LATIN WORD FROM WHICH THEY CAME. ALSO LOOK UP AND WRITE THE MEANING OF THREE OF THE DERIVATIVES THAT YOU DON'T KNOW CLEARLY.

1. benevolence   <u>benevolentia / good will</u>

2. cantata   <u>canto / a vocal and instrumental composition comprising choruses, solos, and recitatives</u>

3. bovine   <u>bos / of, pertaining to, or resembling an ox, cow, or other animal of the genus Bos</u>

4. aural   <u>auris / of, pertaining to, or perceived by the ear.</u>

5. ludicrous   <u>ludus / laughable through obvious absurdity or incongruity.</u>

6. procrastinate   <u>cras / to put off doing something until a future time.</u>

D) Translate these sentences by adding the correct endings to these noun bases and verb stems.

1. The king will give rewards to the hero. Rex premi<u>a</u> her<u>oi</u> da<u>bit</u>.

2. The father is reading the letter out loud to the household. Pater litter<u>as</u> famili<u>ae</u> recita<u>t</u>.

3. A fierce lion is showing (its) teeth to the horse. Leo ferus dent<u>es</u> equ<u>o</u> monstra<u>t</u>.

4. The young man was singing songs for the throng. Adulescens carmin<u>a</u> caterv<u>ae</u> canta<u>bat</u>.

E) Pliny, a Roman scholar, spoke of "cicadae tostae in patellis." Look up any words that you need to in order to translate this. (Tostae is an adjective formed from torreo.)

<u>toasted cicadas (tree crickets) on plates</u>

LESSON 38

A) FIND AN ENGLISH DERIVATIVE FOR EACH OF THESE LATIN WORDS. IN TRYING TO FIND ONE FOR *LITUS*, ITS GENITIVE FORM IS MORE HELPFUL THAN ITS NOMINATIVE.

1. insula	insulate	8. pulcher	pulchritude
2. litus	littoral	9. carcer	incarcerate
3. avis	aviary, aviation	10. canis	canine
4. navis	navy, naval	11. classis	class
5. fatum	fate, fatal	12. bene	benefit, benevolent
6. exemplum	example, exemplary	13. civis	civil
7. periculum	peril	14. significo	significant

B) List in Latin the four adjectives from word list 11.

    1. praeclarus, a, um   3. firmus, a, um

    2. pulcher, pulchra, pulchrum   4. salvus, a, um

C) TRANSLATE THESE PHRASES INTO LATIN. USE THE NOMINATIVE CASE.

1. beautiful island   insula pulchra

2. brilliant citizen   civis praeclarus

3. protected shore   litus salvum

4. beautiful bird   avis pulchra

5. steadfast example   exemplum firmum

Remember that these pairs need to match in gender, number, and case.

D) DO A SYNOPSIS OF *SIGNIFICO* IN THE 3RD PERSON PLURAL.

SIGNIFICO <u>significo, significare, significavi, significatum</u>

present <u>significant</u>

future <u>significabunt</u>

imperfect <u>significabant</u>

E) TRANSLATE THIS: CANIS FIDUS PERICULUM INCOLIS NUNTIABAT. <u>THE FAITHFUL DOG WAS ANNOUNCING THE DANGER TO THE SETTLERS.</u>

LESSON 39

Adjectives and adverbs have similar jobs. They both describe. The difference is in what they describe and what they can tell.

An adjective describes a <u>noun</u> or a <u>pronoun</u>.

It can tell which one, how many, or what kind.

An adverb describes a verb, an adjective, or another adverb. It can tell how, when, where, or to what degree.

A) IN ENGLISH, MANY ADVERBS CAN BE MADE FROM ADJECTIVES BY ADDING -LY. MAKE ADVERBS BY ADDING LY TO THESE ADJECTIVES. YOU WILL HAVE TO MAKE SOME OTHER SMALL CHANGES IN SOME OF THEM (LIKE CHANGING Y TO I).

1. clear	<u>clearly</u>	4. happy	<u>happily</u>
2. steadfast	<u>steadfastly</u>	5. beautiful	<u>beautifully</u>
3. wicked	<u>wickedly</u>	6. kind	<u>kindly</u>

IN LATIN, MANY ADVERBS CAN BE MADE BY ADDING E TO THE BASE OF 1ST AND 2ND DECLENSION ADJECTIVES (THOSE HAVING THE US, A, UM ENDINGS). FORM ADVERBS FROM THESE ADJECTIVES.

1. praeclarus, a, um   <u>praeclare</u>

2. malus, a, um   <u>male</u>

3. firmus, a, um   <u>firme</u>

4. salvus, a, um   <u>salve</u>

5. fidus, a, um   <u>fide</u>

6. pulcher, pulchra, pulchrum   <u>pulchre</u>

B) As a quick review, give the translation of each adjective in its blank.

1. novus   <u>new</u>   2. gratus   <u>grateful</u>

C) Translate these sentences. Label all the adjectives and adverbs.

        adj.   adv.

1. Nauta novus navem fide servat. <u>The new sailor is faithfully saving the ship.</u>

                adv.

2. Dux fabulam grate narrabit. <u>The general will gratefully tell the story.</u>

A very nice thing about Latin adverbs is this: they don't decline!

LESSON 40

A) DECLINE THESE NOUNS ON THE LINES ACCORDING TO THEIR DECLENSIONS. WITH
3RD DECLENSION NOUNS, PAY ATTENTION TO WHETHER OR NOT THEY ARE I-STEMS.

periculum	pericula	praedo	praedones
periculi	periculorum	praedonis	praedonum
periculo	periculis	praedoni	praedonibus
periculum	pericula	praedonem	praedones
periculo	periculis	praedone	praedonibus

navis	naves	litus	litora
navis	navium	litoris	litorum
navi	navibus	litori	litoribus
navem	naves	litus	litora
nave	navibus	litore	litoribus

B) FORM ADVERBS FROM THESE ADJECTIVES AND GIVE THE TRANSLATION FOR EACH
ADVERB.

	ADVERB	TRANSLATION
1. ferus	fere	fiercely
2. peritus	perite	skillfully
3. quietus	quiete	quietly
4. citus	cite	swiftly
5. magnus	magne	greatly
6. acutus	acute	intelligently, sharply
7. bonus	bene	well

*The last one was done for you because "bonus" isn't made into an adverb
in the regular way. (It isn't in English, either, as you can see.)*

C) Placeo is a verb that takes the dative for its object. Study the example below.

Cibus cani placet.   *The food pleases the dog.*
(The food is pleasing to the dog.)

D) Translate these sentences into Latin.

1. The beautiful story pleases the intelligent citizen. <u>Fabula pulchra civi acuto placet.</u>

2. The watchman is quietly announcing the great danger. <u>Custos periculum magnum quiete nuntiat.</u>

3. The fierce storm is badly frightening the new settlers. <u>Tempestas fera incolas novos male terret.</u>

4. Skillful sailors will swiftly save the little ship. <u>Nautae periti navem parvam cite servabunt.</u>

5. Tomorrow they will explore the shore. <u>Litus cras explorabunt.</u>

LESSON 41

A) TRY TO FILL IN THE BLANKS BY YOURSELF WITH THE HELP OF A LATIN DICTIONARY. THE TEACHER MAY SUPPLY SOME HINTS.

1. Piscinarius, i, is related to "pisces," which means <u>fish</u>. A piscinarius is <u>one fond of fish ponds</u>.

2. Artifex, artificis, means <u>craftsman</u>. A likely derivative of this is <u>artifact</u>.

3. Zephyrus, i, means <u>warm west wind</u>. Look up the word "zephyr" in an English dictionary. What does it say? <u>gentle, mild breeze</u>.

4. Lutum, i, is a <u>neuter</u> noun. It means <u>mud, dirt</u>.

5. Vulpes, vulpis, is a <u>noun</u>. This word means <u>fox</u>.

6. Nanus, i, means <u>dwarf</u>. Its accusative singular form is <u>nanum</u>.

7. Zelotypus, a, um, is an <u>adjective</u>. It means <u>jealous</u>.

8. The accusative plural form of sensiculus, i, is <u>sensiculos</u>.

When *ulus* is on the end of a word, that is called a diminutive, i.e, it means little. . . . Sensiculus means little <u>sentence</u>.

9. Pallas, adis, is a <u>proper noun</u>. It is the name of <u>Athena the Greek goddess</u>.

B) LISTED BELOW ARE ENGLISH DERIVATIVES OF WORDS FROM THIS WEEK'S LIST. LOOK THEM UP IN AN ENGLISH DICTIONARY AND WRITE THEIR DEFINITIONS ON THE LINES. WRITE THEIR LATIN SOURCE IN THE PARENTHESES.

1. itinerary   <u>A route or proposed route of a journey</u>   (<u>iter</u>)

2. obscure   <u>dark, hidden, indistinct</u>   (<u>obscurus</u>)

3. mandate	<u>an authoritative command or instruction</u>	(<u>mando</u>)
4. arbor	<u>a shady garden shelter or bower</u>	(<u>arbor</u>)
5. arduous	<u>demanding great care, effort, or labor</u>	(<u>arduus</u>)
6. culmination	<u>the reaching of the highest point or degree</u>	(<u>culmen</u>)

C) WRITE THESE SENTENCES IN LATIN. (SUNTNE SENSICULI? <u>YES</u>)

1. Is the west wind cold? <u>Estne zephyrus gelidus?</u>

2. The craftsman is skillful. <u>Artifex est peritus.</u>

LESSON 42

A) USING ANY VOCABULARY THAT YOU HAVE LEARNED SO FAR, WRITE SIX SENTENCES ACCORDING TO THE PRESCRIPTIONS GIVEN. THEY MUST BE COMPLETE SENTENCES, SO YOU WILL NEED TO INCLUDE OTHER THINGS BESIDES WHAT IS LISTED FOR SOME OF THE SENTENCES. GIVE A GOOD ENGLISH TRANSLATION OF EACH SENTENCE BELOW IT.

1. subject, direct object, adjective

_____

_____

2. subject, predicate nominative

_____

_____

3. subject, direct object, indirect object

_____

_____

4. plural subject, present tense verb, adverb

_____

_____

5. plural subject, future tense verb, adverb

_____

_____

6. subject, imperfect tense verb, adverb, adjective

_____

_____

Label each word that was required.

B) Complete these chants from memory.

M.	F.	N.	M.	F.	N.
hic	haec	hoc	hi	hae	haec
huius	huius	huius	horum	harum	horum
huic	huic	huic	his	his	his
hunc	hanc	hoc	hos	has	haec
hoc	hac	hoc	his	his	his

M.	F.	N.	M.	F.	N.
ille	illa	illud	illi	illae	illa
illius	illius	illius	illorum	illarum	illorum
illi	illi	illi	illis	illis	illis
illum	illam	illud	illos	illas	illa
illo	illa	illo	illis	illis	illis

Here is a new chant to learn.

MASCULINE		FEMININE		NEUTER	
is	ei	ea	eae	id	ea
eius	eorum	eius	earum	eius	eorum
ei	eis	ei	eis	ei	eis
eum	eos	eam	eas	id	ea
eo	eis	ea	eis	eo	eis

LESSON 43

A) FILL IN THE BLANKS.

An ADJECTIVE modifies a <u>noun</u> or a <u>pronoun</u>. It can tell <u>which one</u>, <u>what kind</u>, or <u>how many</u>. A Latin adjective must match the word it modifies in <u>gender</u>, <u>number</u>, and <u>case</u>.

An ADVERB modifies a <u>verb</u>, <u>adjective</u>, or <u>adverb.</u> It can tell <u>to what extent, how</u>, <u>when</u>, or <u>where</u>. The lovely thing about Latin adverbs is that they don't decline.

B) WRITE THE BASE FOR THESE ADJECTIVES IN THE FIRST BLANK, THE CORRESPONDING ADVERB IN THE SECOND BLANK, AND THE TRANSLATION OF THE ADVERB IN THE THIRD BLANK.

	BASE	ADVERB	TRANSLATION
1. longinquus, a, um	<u>longinqu</u>	<u>longinque</u>	<u>distantly</u>
2. novus, a, um	<u>nov</u>	<u>nove</u>	<u>newly</u>
3. gratus, a, um	<u>grat</u>	<u>grate</u>	<u>gratefully</u>
4. fidus, a, um	<u>fid</u>	<u>fide</u>	<u>faithfully</u>

C) MATCH EACH LATIN WORD TO THE CORRECT PART OF SPEECH BY DRAWING A LINE BETWEEN THEM.

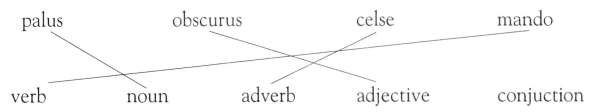

palus   obscurus   celse   mando

verb   noun   adverb   adjective   conjuction

Conjunctions are connecting words. The three conjunctions on this week's list are "sed," "et," and "-que." The dash next to "que" shows that it cannot stand by itself. It is connected to the <u>second</u> thing that is being joined together.

Puellae puerique rident. *The girls and boys are laughing.*

D) TRANSLATE THESE SENTENCES. CIRCLE THE ADVERBS AND UNDERLINE THE CONJUCTIONS IN BOTH LATIN AND ENGLISH.

1. Puella cantabat (pulchre) matri patri<u>que</u>. <u>The girl was singing (beautifully) for (her) mother <u>and</u> father.</u>

2. Dominus pecuniam <u>et</u> navem servo fido mandabit. <u>The master will entrust the money <u>and</u> ship to the faithful servant.</u>

3. Explorator acutus antrum lonquinquum duci monstrabat. <u>The sharp scout was pointing out the far away cave to the general.</u>

4. Explorator (acute) videt <u>sed</u> dux (bene) (non) videt. <u>The scout sees (sharply) but the general does (not) see (well)</u>

5. Antrum magnum duci placet. <u>The large cave pleases the general.</u>

E) TRANSLATE THESE INTO LATIN.

1. The route is steep. <u>Iter est arduum.</u>

2. The bird sings beautifully, but the cow does not sing well. <u>Avis pulchre cantat sed bos non bene cantat.</u>

LESSON 44

THIS STORY IS FOR YOU TO PRACTICE TRANSLATING WITH THE USE OF NOTES THAT WILL HELP YOU GO BEYOND YOUR PRESENT KNOWLEDGE OF LATIN. YOU WILL MEET BOTH VOCABULARY THAT YOU DON'T KNOW AND CONSTRUCTIONS THAT YOU HAVEN'T LEARNED. THE NOTES ARE FOR THE THINGS THAT WOULD BE TOO HARD TO FIGURE OUT. TRANSLATE CAREFULLY THE PARTS THAT YOU KNOW, USE THE NOTES WHERE THEY APPLY, LOOK UP WORDS IN THE DICTIONARY, AND GUESS INTELLIGENTLY ON THE REST.

FABULA PARVA

Olim erat dominus qui mandavit tres margaritas pretiosas famulo fido. Iussit famulum vendere margaritas mercatori in urbe longinqua. Famulus incipit iter cum margaritis obscuris in vestem. Cum ambulavisset mille passus, latrones mali oppugnaverunt. Famulus erat citior quam latrones et sic evasit. Cum ambulavisset duo milia passuum, leones feri oppugnaverunt. Arborem ascendit et sic evasit. Cum ambulavisset tria milia passuum, nox circumdedit tenebras famulo fido et in paludem cecidit. Clamavit et comes clamorem audivit. Comes funem iecit et sic famulus evasit. Cum ambulavisset quattuor milia passuum, ad litus pervenit. Navem conscendit ut veheretur ad urbem ubi mercator vixit. Cum vectus esset nave quinque milia passuum, praedones improbi oppugnaverunt navem, sed famulus saluit de nave et navit ad harenam et sic evasit. Famulus fidus et defessus ad urbem tandem pervenit. Dixit, "Ecce! Salvus sum et margaritae sunt salvae. Nunc possum vendere margaritas et ferre pecuniam ad dominum meum. Si hic thesaurus fuisset gravior et maior, non pervenissemus salve." Mercator visit margaritas esse pretiosissimas et dixit, "Dabo magnum saccum auri pro margaritas." Famulus dixit, "Eheu!"

FINIS

iussit	he ordered (iubeo, iubere, iussi, iussum)
cum margaritis	*cum* means something different here than it does in the rest of the story
cum ambulavisset	when he had walked
mille passus	a mile (a thousand paces)
evasit	he escaped (evado, evadere, evasi, evasum)
cecidit	he fell (cado, cadere, cecidi, casum)
iecit	he threw (iacio, iacere, ieci, iactum)
ut veheretur	in order to sail
cum vectus esset nave	when he had sailed
saluit	he jumped (salio, salire, salui, saltum)
navit	he swam (no, nare, navi)
dixit	he said (dico, dicere, dixi, dictum)
Si . . . fuisset gravior et maior	If . . . had been heavier and bigger

There once was a master who entrusted three costly pearls to a faithful servant. He ordered the servant to sell the pearls to a merchant in a distant city. The servant began the journey with the pearls hidden in his clothing. When he had walked a mile, evil robbers attacked. The servant was swifter than the robbers and thus he escaped. When he had walked two miles fierce lions attacked. He climbed a tree and thus he escaped. When he had walked three miles night surrounded the faithful servant with darkness and he fell in a swamp. He shouted and a fellow-traveler heard the shout. The fellow-traveller threw a rope and thus the servant escaped. When he had walked four miles he arrived at the shore. He boarded a ship in order to sail to the city where the merchant lived. When he had sailed five miles, wicked pirates attacked the ship, but the servant jumped down from the ship and swam to the beach and thus he escaped. The faithful and weary servant finally arrived at the city. He said "Behold! I am safe and the pearls are safe. Now I am able to sell the pearls and bring the money to my master.

If this treasure had been heavier and bigger, we would not have arrived safely." The merchant saw that the pearls were very costly and said, "I will give you a big bag of gold in exchange for the pearls. The servant said, "Woe!"

EXTRA NOTES: (TEACHER'S NOTE NOT IN STUDENT TEXT)

Most of the verbs in the story are in the perfect tense.

Iubeo takes an infinitive phrase: the subject in the accusative and the verb in the infinitive form.

Ambulavisset, vectus esset, fuisset, pervenissemus are all in the subjunctive mood.

Mercator visit. . . . What follows is an indirect statement which uses an infinitive phrase.

LESSON 45

A) WRITE THE ENDING CHANTS FOR THESE DECLENSIONS.

1ST DECLENSION

a	ae
(ae)	(arum)
ae	is
am	as
a	is

2ND DECLENSION

us	i	um	a
(i)	(orum)	(i)	(orum)
o	is	o	is
um	os	um	a
o	is	o	is

3RD DECLENSION

x	es
(is)	(um)
i	ibus
em	es
e	ibus

In the chants above, circle the genitive endings in each (both singular and plural).

B) THE GENITIVE CASE IS USED TO SHOW POSSESSION. IT CAN BE TRANSLATED WITH "OF" OR WITH AN APOSTROPHE, E.G. PUELLAE = "OF THE GIRL" OR "THE GIRL'S."

Translate these nouns in the genitive case. Translate some of them with "of" and some of them with an apostrophe.

1. arboris   <u>of the tree/the tree's</u>

2. carceris   <u>the prison's/of the prison</u>

3. coniugis   <u>the husband's *or* the wife's/of the husband *or* of the wife</u>

4. oppidi   <u>of the town/the town's</u>

5. herois   <u>the hero's/of the hero</u>

6. linguae   <u>of the language/the language's</u>

7. filiae   <u>the daughter's/of the daughter</u>

8. mercatoris   <u>the merchant's/of the merchant</u>

C) FILL IN THE BLANKS WITH CASE AND NUMBER.

In the 1ST DECLENSION, the genitive singular form is the same as the <u>dative singular</u> and the <u>nominative plural</u>.

In the 2ND DECLENSION (except for neuter nouns) the genitive singular form is the same as the <u>nominative plural</u>.

LESSON 46

A) TRANSLATE THESE GENITIVE FORMS USING "OF." PAY ATTENTION TO WHETHER THE FORMS ARE SINGULAR OR PLURAL.

1. famis   of famine

2. mortis   of death

3. divitiarum   of riches

4. librorum   of the books

5. vallis   of the valley

B) TRANSLATE THESE GENITIVE FORMS USING AN APOSTROPHE. DON'T FORGET TO NOTICE WHETHER THEY ARE SINGULAR OR PLURAL.

1. pastoris   the shepherd's

2. leonum   the lions'

3. pastorum   the shepherds'

4. librorum   the books'

5. bovis   the cow's

C) GIVE THESE ADVERBS IN LATIN.

1. harshly   aspere

2. yesterday   heri

3. justly   iuste

4. gratefully   grate

D) TRANSLATE *WHITE BIRD* INTO LATIN AND DECLINE IT.

avis alba	aves albae
avis albae	avium albarum
avi albae	avibus albis
avem albam	aves albas
ave alba	avibus albis

E) TRANSLATE THESE SENTENCES. WHEN TRANSLATING THE GENITIVE FORM CONSIDER WHETHER IT WOULD BE BEST TO USE "OF" OR AN APOSTROPHE.

1. Pastor ovium vestigia leonis demonstrabat. The shepherd of the sheep was pointing out the tracks of the lion.

2. Mors ovis pastori non placet. The death of the sheep does not please the shepherd.

3. Virtus constantiaque pastoris gregem servabunt. The courage and steadfastness of the shepherd will save the flock.

4. Agricolae canis ululabat heri. The farmer's dog was howling yesterday.

LESSON 47

A) COMPLETE THIS CHANT, LABELING THE CASES ON THE LINES TO THE RIGHT.

ego	nos	NOMINATIVE
mei	nostrum	GENITIVE
mihi	nobis	DATIVE
me	nos	ACCUSATIVE
me	nobis	ABLATIVE
tu	vos	NOMINATIVE
tui	vestrum	GENITIVE
tibi	vobis	DATIVE
te	vos	ACCUSATIVE
te	vobis	ABLATIVE

B) CONJUGATE *SUM* IN THE PRESENT, FUTURE, AND IMPERFECT TENSES.

PRESENT		FUTURE		IMPERFECT	
sum	sumus	ero	erimus	eram	eramus
es	estis	eris	eritis	eras	eratis
est	sunt	erit	erunt	erat	erant

C) TRANSLATE THESE SENTENCES. ALL OF THEM CONTAIN PREDICATE NOMINATIVES OR PREDICATE ADJECTIVES. UNDERLINE THE PREDICATE NOMINATIVES AND CIRCLE THE PREDICATE ADJECTIVES.

1. Tu eras asper. You were (harsh.)

2. Adulescens erit pastor. The young man will be a shepherd.

3. Viri sunt agricolae. The men are farmers.

4. Ovis est alba. <u>The sheep is (white).</u>

5. Nimbi erant nigri. <u>The clouds were (black).</u>

6. Eras asper. <u>You were (harsh).</u>

What is the difference between the first sentence and the last? <u>Although they both contain "you," it is emphasized in the first sentence.</u>

LESSON 48

A) TRANSLATE THESE SENTENCES INTO LATIN. BE CAREFUL TO MATCH THE PREDICATE ADJECTIVE TO THE SUBJECT IN GENDER, NUMBER, AND CASE.

1. The hiding place was secure. Latebra erat salva.

2. Lions are fierce. Leones sunt feri.

3. The footprints were new. Vestigia erant nova.

4. The shepherd's courage is great. Virtus pastoris est magna.

5. The white cliffs are far away. Scopuli albi sunt longinqui.

B) DERIVATIVES OF THE WORDS FROM WORD LIST 13 ABOUND. FIND A DERIVATIVE APIECE FOR 15 OF THE WORDS.

1. fames—famine, famished

2. pastor—pastor, pastoral

3. ovis—ovine

4. leo—leonine

5. virtus—virtual, virtue, virtuous, virtuoso

6. mors—mortal, mortuary

7. vestigium—vestige, vestigial

8. constantia—constant, constancy

9. vulnero—vulnerable

10. vexo—vex

11. urgeo—urge, urgent, urgency

12. impendeo—impending

13. albus—albumen, albino, album

14. niger—Nigeria

15. asper—asperity, asperate

Lesson 49

A) In each sentence label the nouns, which are in bold face, according to whether they are a subject, direct object, or predicate nominative. You may abbreviate. Translate the sentences on the lines.

      S.   P.N.

1. **Adulescens** erit **agricola**. <u>The young man will be a farmer.</u>

    S.   P.N.

2. **Vir** est **custos**. <u>The man is a guard.</u>

    S.   D.O.

3. **Leo gregem** vexabat. <u>The lion was harassing the flock/herd.</u>

    D.O.   S.

4. **Agricolam imber** delectat. <u>The rain shower delights the farmer.</u>

B) These are excerpts from the Vulgate. See how many of them you can translate.

1. " Ego sum pastor bonus. Bonus pastor animam suam dat pro ovibus." <u>"I am the good shepherd. The good shepherd gives his own life for the sheep."</u>

2. "Vos de mundo hoc estis, ego non sum de hoc mundo." <u>"You are of this world, I am not of this world."</u>

3. " Ego sum resurrectio et vita." <u>"I am the resurrection and the life."</u>

4. "Dicit ei Iesus: 'Ego sum via, et veritas, et vita: nemo venit ad Patrem, nisi per me.'" "Jesus said to him: 'I am the way, and the truth, and the life: no one comes to the Father, except through me.'"

5. "Ego sum lux mundi: qui sequitur me, non ambulabit in tenebris, sed habebit lucem vitae." "I am the light of the world: he who follows me will not walk in darkness, but will have the light of life.

6. "Ego sum vitis vera, et Pater meus agricola est. . . . Ego sum vitis, vos palmites: qui manet in me, et ego in eo, hic fert fructum multum: quia sine me nihil potestis facere." " I am the true vine, and my Father is the farmer. . . . I am the vine, you (are) the branches: he who remains in me, and I in him, this one brings forth much fruit: because without me you are able to do nothing.

7. "Ego sum panis vitae" "I am the bread of life."

Lesson 50

A) *The <u>genitive</u> case is used for possession.*

Give the declension and translation of these nouns in the genitive case.
The first one is done for you.

1. viri (2)   the man's

2. divitiarum (<u>1</u>)   <u>of the riches</u>

3. ovium (<u>3</u>)   <u>of the sheep</u>

4. pastoris (<u>3</u>)   <u>of the shepherd</u>

5. leonum (<u>3</u>)   <u>the lions'</u>

6. canis (<u>3</u>)   <u>the dog's</u>

7. praedonum (<u>3</u>)   <u>the pirates'</u>

8. navis (<u>3</u>)   <u>of the ship</u>

B) *The <u>dative</u> case is used for indirect objects. "To" and "for" can be used to translate this.*

Translate these.

1. Adulescens vestigium leonis pastori significabat. <u>The young man was pointing out the footprint of the lion to the shepherd.</u>

2. Imber heri impendebat. <u>A rainstorm was threatening yesterday.</u>

3. Vir famulo divitias mandabit. <u>The man will entrust the riches to the slave.</u>

4. Nos gregem hodie urgebamus. <u>We were pressing hard the flock today.</u>

C) Give a synopsis of *vulnero* in the 3rd person singular.

VULNERO <u>vulnero, vulnerare, vulneravi, vulneratum</u>

      present <u>vulnerat</u>

      future <u>vulnerabit</u>

      imperfect <u>vulnerabat</u>

D) Mors is an example of another kind of 3rd declension noun that is an i-stem. The rule for this kind is that its nominative form ends in "s" or "x" and its base ends with two consonants. There is also one example of this group in each of word lists 1, 2, and 4. Decline mors and one of the others that fits in this category.

mors	<u>mortes</u>	<u>dens</u>	<u>dentes</u>
mortis	<u>mortium</u>	<u>dentis</u>	<u>dentium</u>
<u>morti</u>	<u>mortibus</u>	<u>denti</u>	<u>dentibus</u>
<u>mortem</u>	<u>mortes</u>	<u>dentem</u>	<u>dentes</u>
<u>morte</u>	<u>mortibus</u>	<u>dente</u>	<u>dentibus</u>

<u>serpens</u>	<u>serpentes</u>	<u>fons</u>	<u>fontes</u>
<u>serpentis</u>	<u>serpentium</u>	<u>fontis</u>	<u>fontium</u>
<u>serpenti</u>	<u>serpentibus</u>	<u>fonti</u>	<u>fontibus</u>
<u>serpentem</u>	<u>serpentes</u>	<u>fontem</u>	<u>fontes</u>
<u>serpente</u>	<u>serpentibus</u>	<u>fonte</u>	<u>fontibus</u>

LESSON 51

A) TRANSLATE USING THE BEING VERB IN THESE SENTENCES.

1. Coniunx est mercator. <u>The husband is a merchant.</u>

2. Viri non sunt civespatriae. <u>The men are not citizens of the native land.</u>

3. Culmen erit meta. <u>The peak will be the turning point.</u>

4. Insula erat latebra. <u>The island was a hideout.</u>

5. Canis est custos. <u>The dog is the guard.</u>

6. Leones sunt feri. <u>The lions are fierce.</u>

7. Vestigia leonum sunt nova. <u>The tracks of the lions are new.</u>

8. Pastores erunt fidi. <u>The shepherds will be faithful.</u>

9. Imber erat gelidus. <u>The rain was like ice.</u>

10. Viri erant laeti. <u>The men were happy.</u>

B) YOU HAVE LEARNED TWO WORDS THAT MEAN "MAN": VIR MEANS "A MALE PERSON" AND HOMO MEANS "A HUMAN BEING." CHOOSE AN ADJECTIVE TO GO WITH EACH AND DECLINE BOTH WORDS WITH THEIR ADJECTIVES IN THE BOXES. TAKE NOTE OF THE STEM OF HOMO; YOU HAVEN'T MET IT BEFORE.

vir <u>iustus (e.g.)</u>	<u>viri iusti</u>
viri <u>iusti</u>	<u>virorum iustorum</u>
<u>viro iusto</u>	<u>viris iustis</u>
<u>virum iustum</u>	<u>viros iustos</u>
<u>viro iusto</u>	<u>viris iustis</u>

homo <u>gratus</u>	<u>homines grati</u>
hominis <u>grati</u>	<u>hominum gratorum</u>
<u>homini grato</u>	<u>hominibus gratis</u>
<u>hominem gratum</u>	<u>homines gratos</u>
<u>homine grato</u>	<u>hominibus gratis</u>

LESSON 52

A) TRANSLATE THESE WORDS IN THE GENITIVE CASE INTO ENGLISH.

1. ovium   <u>of the sheep</u>

2. patris   <u>the father's</u>

3. coniugis   <u>the husband's or wife's</u>

4. famularum   <u>the female slaves'</u>

5. iudicis   <u>the judge's</u>

6. mulierum   <u>the women's</u>

B) TRANSLATE THESE INTO LATIN.

1. men's   <u>virorum</u>

2. citizen's   <u>civis</u>

3. mothers'   <u>matrum</u>

4. flock's   <u>gregis</u>

5. young men's   <u>adulescentium</u>

C) TRANSLATE THESE SENTENCES INTO ENGLISH.

1. Oves pastoris boni sunt salvae. <u>The good shepherd's sheep are safe.</u>

2. Magister egregius discipulos perite docebat. <u>The outstanding teacher was skillfully teaching the students.</u>

3. Deus vivus nos servabit. <u>The living God will save us.</u>

4. Lux lunae stellarumque est pulchra. <u>The light of the moon and stars is beautiful.</u>

5. Divitias et laudem hominum non amant. <u>They do not love riches and the praise of men.</u>

6. Testimonium custodis honesti reum damnabit. <u>The testimony of the honest watchman will condemn the defendant.</u>

7. Virtus constantiaque viri comites servabunt. <u>The courage and stead-fastness of the man will save the companions.</u>

8. Carmina virginum turbam delectabant. <u>The songs of the maidens were delighting the crowd.</u>

D) TRANSLATE THESE INTO LATIN.

1. The scout was approaching the top of the lofty mountain. <u>Explorator ad culmen montis celsi appropinquabat.</u>

2. The prison was a gloomy place. <u>Carcer erat tenebrosus.</u>

3. Darkness is hiding the robbers' ambush, but the hero will avoid the danger. <u>Tenebrae insidias latronum occultant, sed heros periculum vitabit.</u>

LESSON 53

A) Translate the verbs as they are read. On the line to the left of the number, indicate the tense by writing "p" for present, "f" for future, and "i" for imperfect.

[(Teacher's note—not in Student text) Latin verbs to be read:

1. cantabam   2. mandabit   3. mutant   4. vitas   5. dabunt

6. peccabant 7. ridebamus 8. hiemabimus 9. clamabatis 10. accusabat]

1. I was singing	i	6. they were sinning	i
2. he will entrust	f	7. we were laughing	i
3. they are changing	p	8. we shall spend the winter	f
4. you avoid	p	9. you all were shouting	i
5. they will give	f	10. he was accusing	i

B) Write the four principal parts of amo on the lines below.

1. amo   2. amare   3. amavi   4. amatum

The three tenses you have used so far have all used the present stem; circle the present stem of "amo" in the principal parts that you wrote above.

Taking the "i" from the 3rd principal part gives you the perfect stem. The perfect stem of "amo" is "amav." Find that above and circle it. Now, notice how it is used to form the perfect tense and how that tense is translated.

[Student Text has the rest of "B)" on the previous page.]

amavi	I loved, I have loved, I did love
amavisti	you loved, you have loved, you did love
amavit	he, she, or it loved, did love, have loved
amavimus	we loved, have loved, did love
amavistis	you all loved, did love, have loved
amaverunt	they have loved, did love, loved

C) TRANSLATE THESE SENTENCES USING THE PERFECT TENSE.

1. Legio oppugnavit. <u>The legion attacked.</u>

2. Mulier accusavit. <u>The woman accused.</u>

3. Oves erraverunt. <u>The sheep have wandered.</u>

LESSON 54

A) MARK THE LINE NEXT TO ANY OF THESE 3RD DECLENSION NOUNS THAT ARE I-STEMS. BE READY TO EXPLAIN WHY YOU THINK SO.

1. __x__   turris, turris   4. _____   vesper, vesperis

2. __x__   pons, pontis   5. __x__   urbs, urbis

3. _____   legio, legionis   6. _____   vox, vocis

B) CONJUGATE *POSTULO* IN THE PERFECT TENSE AND TRANSLATE IT.

I demanded	postulavi	postulavimus	we demanded
you demanded	postulavisti	postulavistis	you (all) demanded
he, she, it demanded	postulavit	postulaverunt	they demanded

Explain how you find the perfect stem: Remove the "i" from the 3rd principal part.

C) YOU ALREADY KNOW THAT THE ACCUSATIVE CASE IS USED FOR DIRECT OBJECTS. IT IS ALSO USED FOR THE OBJECTS OF SOME PREPOSITIONS. THREE OF THOSE PREPOSITIONS ARE "PER," "TRANS," AND "IN" WHEN "IN" MEANS "INTO." IN THE EXAMPLES, THE OBJECT OF THE PREPOSITION IS UNDERLINED.

1. per limen   (through the doorway)

2. in urbem   (into the city)

3. trans viam   (across the road)

D) TRANSLATE THESE SENTENCES.

1. Legio defessa in provinciam erravit. <u>The weary legion wandered into the province.</u>

2. Victor copias trans regionem vexavit. <u>The victor harassed the troops across the region.</u>

3. Fulmen per montes sonavit. <u>The thunderbolt resounded through the mountains.</u>

4. Miles amicum in urbem portavit. <u>The soldier has carried the friend into the city.</u>

E) COMPLETE THESE CHANTS FROM MEMORY.

i	imus	ero	erimus	eram	eramus
isti	istis	eris	eritis	eras	eratis
it	erunt	erit	erint	erat	erant

F) *TRANS* HAS MANY ENGLISH DERIVATIVES. ADD AS MANY TO THIS LIST AS YOU CAN AND THEN CHOOSE ONE TO GIVE ITS ETYMOLOGY: TRANSPORT, TRANSLATE, TRANSGRESS, <u>TRANSCRIBE, TRANSDUCER, TRANSFER, TRANSIT, TRANSLITERATE, TRANS-MIT, TRANSVERSE</u>

ETYMOLOGY:

_____

_____

_____

_____

LESSON 55

A) TRANSLATE THESE INTO LATIN.

1. The hiding place of the robbers was distant. <u>Latebra latronum erat longingua.</u>

2. The strength of the shepherd is great. <u>Virtus pastoris est magna.</u>

3. The law of the native land is just. <u>Lex patriae est iusta.</u>

4. The buildings of the city will be beautiful. <u>Aedificia urbis erunt pulchra.</u>

B) DECLINE *LEGIO* AND *LIMEN* ON THE LINES. *LIMEN* IS A NEUTER NOUN AND HAS THE CHARACTERISTICS OF ALL NEUTER NOUNS: THE NOMINATIVE AND ACCUSATIVE FORMS ARE THE SAME IN BOTH SINGULAR AND PLURAL, AND THE PLURAL NOMINATIVE ENDING IS "A".

legio	<u>legiones</u>	limen	<u>limina</u>
<u>legionis</u>	<u>legionum</u>	<u>liminis</u>	<u>liminum</u>
<u>legioni</u>	<u>legionibus</u>	<u>limini</u>	<u>liminibus</u>
<u>legionem</u>	<u>legiones</u>	<u>limen</u>	<u>limina</u>
<u>legione</u>	<u>legionibus</u>	<u>limine</u>	<u>liminibus</u>

C) TRANSLATE THESE VERBS AND GIVE THE PERSON AND NUMBER FOR EACH.

	TRANSLATION	PERSON	NUMBER
1. accusavi	<u>I accused</u>	<u>1st person</u>	<u>singular</u>
2. erravisti	<u>you wandered</u>	<u>2nd person</u>	<u>singular</u>

3. stetit	he stood	3rd person	singular
4. postulavimus	we have demanded	1st person	plural
5. oppugnaverunt	they did attack	3rd person	plural
6. ursistis	you (all) pressed hard	2nd person	plural

D) FILL IN THE BLANKS ABOUT TYPES OF SOLDIERS.

Eques, equitis is a word that you learned in the last book. It means horse-man and is obviously related to the word for horse: equus

Pedes, peditis is a word that you have not yet learned. It is related to *pes, pedis* in the same way that *eques* is related to the word for horse. What does *pes* mean? foot

What would *pedes* mean? footsoldier

LESSON 56

A) TRANSLATE THESE VERBS INTO LATIN AND GIVE THEIR TENSES.

	TRANSLATION	TENSE
1. you have stood	stetisti	perfect
2. you did stand	stetisti	perfect
3. you stood	stetisti	perfect
4. I am accusing	accuso	present
5. they accused	accusaverunt	perfect
6. he is mistaken	errat	present
7. it is standing	stat	present
8. we demanded	postulavimus	perfect
9. they will attack	oppugnabunt	future
10. you (all) gave	dedistis	perfect

B) TRANSLATE THESE SENTENCES.

1. Nautae per gurgites heri navigaverunt. The sailors sailed through the whirlpools yesterday.

2. Classis per angustias navigabit hodie. The fleet will sail through the narrows today.

3. Turres castelli trans aquam possum videre. I am able to see the turrets of the castle across the water.

4. Potesne videre castellum nunc? Are you able to see the castle now?

C) THIS WILL BE YOUR LAST NEW CHANT IN THIS BOOK. THERE ARE MANY LITTLE WORDS IN LATIN THAT START WITH "Q," AND IF YOU MEMORIZE THESE WELL NOW, IT WILL CONTRIBUTE TO YOUR HAPPINESS AS A LATIN SCHOLAR.

MASCULINE		FEMININE		NEUTER	
qui	qui	quae	quae	quod	quae
cuius	quorum	cuius	quarum	cuius	quorum
cui	quibus	cui	quibus	cui	quibus
quem	quos	quam	quas	quod	quae
quo	quibus	qua	quibus	quo	quibus

COMPLETE THIS CHANT FROM MEMORY.

MASCULINE		FEMININE		NEUTER	
is	ei	ea	eae	id	ea
eius	eorum	eius	earum	eius	eorum
ei	eis	ei	eis	ei	eis
eum	eos	eam	eas	id	ea
eo	eis	ea	eis	eo	eis

LESSON 57

A) CONJUGATE *ERRO* IN THE PERFECT TENSE AND TRANSLATE IT.

I wandered	erravi	erravimus	we wandered
you wandered	erravisti	erravistis	you all wandered
he wandered	erravit	erraverunt	they wandered

B) GIVE A SYNOPSIS FOR EACH OF THESE VERBS AS PRESCRIBED.

OPPUGNO oppugnare, oppugnavi, oppugnatum

    first person singular

        present oppugno

        future oppugnabo

        imperfect oppugnabam

        perfect oppugnavi

POSTULO postulare, postulavi, postulatum

    first person plural

        present postulamus

        future postulabimus

        imperfect postulabamus

        perfect postulavimus

C) TRANSLATE THESE SENTENCES.

1. Legio urbem parvam non oppugnavit. The legion did not attack the unimportant city.

2. Tecta urbis stant. <u>The city's buildings stand.</u>

3. Legio prima non erat parva. <u>The first legion was not small.</u>

ANSWER THESE QUESTIONS ABOUT THE SENTENCES:

What tense is *oppugnavit*? <u>perfect</u> What tense is *erat*? <u>imperfect</u>

What is the adverb used in those sentences? <u> non </u> What case is *urbis* in #2? <u>genitive</u>

In #3, *prima* and *parva* are both <u>adjectives</u>. *Parva* is a <u>predicate adjective</u>.

D) TRY YOUR HAND AT TRANSLATING THESE INTO LATIN.

1. The small fleet wandered through the islands. <u>Parva classis per insulas erravit.</u>

2. The foremost city of the native land was beautiful. <u>Prima urbs patriae erat pulchra.</u>

3. The rumor of war will frighten the small city. <u>Fama belli parvam urbem terrebit.</u>

FOR YOUR INFORMATION

The legion was the major unit of the Roman army consisting of 3,000 to 6,000 infantry troops and 100 to 200 cavalrymen. In the early years of the Empire, there were 28 legions and each one had its own traditions and pride. The 10th legion won recognition as the favorite unit of Julius Caesar. Later, in Augustus Caesar's reign, German tribes devastated three legions under the command of the consul Quintilius Varus. Augustus is quoted by Suetonius as saying "Quintili Vare, legiones redde." Those three legions weren't replaced until half a century later, and the number of legions grew after that to deal with threats on the frontier.

LESSON 58

A) GIVE A SYNOPSIS OF *STO* IN THE THIRD PERSON PLURAL.

STO <u>sto, stare, steti, statum</u>

   present <u>stant</u>

   future <u>stabunt</u>

   imperfect <u>stabant</u>

   perfect <u>steterunt</u>

B) CROSS OUT THE INCORRECT TRANSLATION IN EACH SET.

1. accusavi
  I have accused   ~~*I shall accuse*~~   *I accused*

2. postulaverunt
  ~~*you(all) have accused*~~   *they have accused*   *they did accuse*

3. erravimus
  ~~*we were wandering*~~   *we have wandered*   *we wandered*

4. oppugnavistis
  you(all) attacked   *you(all) have attacked*   ~~*he attacked*~~

5. stetit
  he stood   ~~*he was standing*~~   *he has stood*

C) WRITE THREE CORRECT TRANSLATIONS FOR THIS VERB.

cantavisti   <u>you sang</u>   <u>you did sing</u>   <u>you have sung</u>

D) Translate these sentences.

1. Aedificia urbis semper non stabunt. <u>The city's buildings will not always stand.</u>

2. Coniunx cenam hospitibus parabat. <u>The wife was preparing dinner for the guests.</u>

3. Vir defessus trans limen ambulavit. <u>The weary man walked across the threshold.</u>

4. Turres urbis longinquae lucent et exploratores delectant. <u>The towers of the distant city shine and delight the explorers.</u>

Answer these questions about the sentences:

What case is *urbis* in #1 and #4? <u>genitive</u>

What are the gender, case, and number of *defessus* in #3? <u>masculine, nominative, singular</u>

What part of speech is *semper*? <u>adverb</u>

What case is *hospitibus* in #2? <u>dative</u>

E) Translate these sentences into Latin.

1. The lion attacked the small flock. <u>Leo gregem parvum oppugnavit.</u>

2. A famine threatened the great city. <u>Fames urbem magnam impendit.</u>

3. The master put watchmen around the building. <u>Dominus custodes tecto circumdedit.</u>

Lesson 59

A) Conjugate *sto* in the perfect tense and give the translations on the sides.

I stood	STETI	STETIMUS	we stood
you stood	STETISTI	STETISTIS	you (all) stood
he, she, it stood	STETIT	STETERUNT	they stood

B) Find the perfect stem of these verbs by using the rule that you've learned. Begin by writing the principal parts of the verbs from memory if you can.

	PRINCIPAL PARTS	PERFECT STEM
1. urgeo	urgere, ursi	urs
2. doceo	docere, docui, doctum	docu
3. rideo	ridere, risi, risum	ris
4. do	dare, dedi, datum	ded
5. candeo	candere, candui	candu

C) Translate these sentences.

1. The soldier urged his horse through the river. Miles equum per fluvium ursit.

2. The master taught the ignorant male servant the laws of the native land. Dominus famulō ignarō leges patriae docuit.

3. The woman gave grain to the slaves. Femina frumentum servis dedit.

4. Puella laeta *saepe risit. <u>The happy girl often laughed.</u>

D) Give this synopsis of accuso in the 2nd person plural

ACCUSO <u>accuso, accusare, accusavi, accusatum</u>

> *present* <u>accusatis</u>
>
> *future* <u>accusabitis</u>
>
> *imperfect* <u>accusabatis</u>
>
> *perfect* <u>accusavistis</u>

E) Below are some compound verbs formed by adding prefixes to *sto*. Think what the meaning of the verb might be and write your guess on the first line. Then look it up in a Latin dictionary and write the definition which you find there on the second line.

1. asto(adsto)

   <u>stand near, stand by</u>

2. exsto (exto)

   <u>stand out, project, be visible</u>

3. resto

   <u>remain, be left over</u>

4. insto

   <u>press on, be near</u>

*This is a word that you learned in the first book. It is not a form of *saepes, is.*

Lesson 60

A) Find the Latin verbs in the first column that correctly translate the English in the second column and write them in the corresponding blanks.

1. cantavi	1. he avoided	vitavit
2. vulneraverunt	2. they wound	vulnerant
3. portavisti	3. they did report	nuntiaverunt
4. vitavit	4. you carried	portavisti
5. rogavimus	5. he manages	administrat
6. hiemavimus	6. he sets free	liberat
7. nuntiaverunt	7. I sang	cantavi
8. agitabas	8. I entered	intravi
9. paraverunt	9. he ordered	imperavit
10. administrat	10. we asked	rogavimus
11. recuperavistis	11. they did wound	vulneraverunt
12. liberat	12. you(all) have recovered	recuperavistis
13. vulnerant	13. you were disturbing	agitabas
14. imperavit	14. they prepared	paraverunt
15. intravi	15. we spent the winter	hiemavimus

B) Translate these sentences.

1. Nuntius citus litteras trans regionem heri portavit. Yesterday, the swift messenger carried the letter across the region.

2. Luna per fenestram lucebat. <u>The moon was shining through the window.</u>

3. Nautae defessi in locum quietum navigaverunt. <u>The weary sailors sailed into the quiet place.</u>

4. The weary father walked safely through the doorway. <u>Pater defessus per limen salve ambulavit.</u>

5. The merchant approached the first dwellings of the city. <u>Mercator ad prima tecta urbis appropinquavit.</u>

LESSON 61

A) GIVE THE CASE USED FOR EACH OF THESE FUNCTIONS. YOU WILL DO THE LAST ONE WITH TWO BLANKS LATER.

subject	nominative
direct object	accusative
predicate nominative	nominative
indirect object	dative
showing possession	genitive
object of prepositions (per, trans, and in=into)	accusative
place where	ablative

B) A CASE YOU HAVE NOT USED IN SENTENCES YET IS THE ABLATIVE CASE. IT HAS MANY USES, MORE THAN YOU WANT TO KNOW ABOUT RIGHT NOW. ONE USE IS TO TELL THE PLACE WHERE THE SENTENCE IS HAPPENING. THE LATIN PREPOSITION *IN* IS USED WITH THIS AND IS TRANSLATED AS "IN" OR "ON." NOTE IN THE EXAMPLES THAT THE UNDERLINED WORD IS THE PLACE AND IS IN THE ABLATIVE CASE.

Vir in limine stabat.   The man was standing in the doorway.

Pastor oves in agro spectat.   The shepherd is watching the sheep in the field.

In insula errabant.   They were wandering on the island.

C) TRANSLATE THESE PHRASES INTO LATIN.

1. on the roof   in tecto

2. in the city   <u>in urbe</u>

3. in the tower   <u>in turre</u>

4. in the hideout   <u>in latebra</u>

5. on the ship   <u>in nave</u>

6. in the valleys   <u>in vallibus</u>

D) TRANSLATE THESE SENTENCES.

1. Frumentum in agris torret. <u>The grain in the fields is burning.</u>

2. Incolae in montibus explorabunt. <u>The settlers will explore in the mountains.</u>

3. Mercator cibum in via portat. <u>The merchant is carrying food on the road.</u>

Now finish "A" above, writing "place where" on the left and ablative for the case.

LESSON 62

A) CONJUGATE AND TRANSLATE *COMPLEO* IN THE PERFECT TENSE.

I filled	COMPLEVI	COMPLEVIMUS	we filled
you filled	COMPLEVISTI	COMPLEVISTIS	you (all) filled
he, she, or it filled	COMPLEVIT	COMPLEVERUNT	they filled

B) TRANSLATE THESE PHRASES INTO ENGLISH, PAYING CAREFUL ATTENTION TO THE CASE OF THE NOUN THAT FOLLOWS THE PREPOSITION *IN*. IF IT IS IN THE ABLATIVE, *IN* MEANS <u>IN</u> OR <u>ON</u>, BUT IF IT IS IN THE ACCUSATIVE, *IN* MEANS <u>INTO</u>.

1. in vallo	on the wall		4. in culmine	on the peak
2. in urbem	into the city		5. in litore	on the shore
3. in viam	into the road		6. in carcerem	into prison

C) DECLINE *IUVENIS* ON THE LINES.

iuvenis	iuvenes
iuvenis	iuvenium
iuveni	iuvenibus
iuvenem	iuvenes
iuvene	iuvenibus

D) TRANSLATE THESE SENTENCES INTO ENGLISH.

1. Mare in harena caluit. <u>The sea was warm on the beach.</u>

2. Nepos senis in provincia superat. <u>The grandson of the old man is conquering in the province.</u>

3. Securis in vallo iacebat. <u>The axe was lying on the wall.</u>

4. Explorator vestigium in silva videbit. <u>The scout will see the footprint in the forest.</u>

E) COMPLETE THIS CHANT:

duco   <u>ducimus</u>

<u>ducis</u>   <u>ducitis</u>

<u>ducit</u>   <u>ducunt</u>

LESSON 63

A) THE THIRD, AND LAST, GROUP OF I-STEMS IN THE 3RD DECLENSION ARE NEUTER NOUNS THAT END IN *E, AL,* AND *AR.* THERE ARE TWO EXAMPLES OF THIS GROUP ON THIS WEEK'S LIST. AFTER EXAMINING THE DECLENSION OF *MARE,* FOLLOW THAT PATTERN TO DECLINE THE OTHER ONE IN THIS WEEK'S LIST. (N.B. THE "I" SHOWS UP MORE IN THIS KIND OF I-STEM THAN IN THE OTHERS, AND THESE NOUNS STILL HAVE THE USUAL CHARACTERISTICS OF NEUTER NOUNS. CIRCLE ALL THE PLACES THAT THE EXTRA "I" SHOWS UP.)

mare	maria	animal	animalia
maris	marium	animalis	animalium
mari	maribus	animali	animalibus
mare	maria	animal	animalia
mari	maribus	animali	animalibus

B) DO A SYNOPSIS OF *SUPERO* IN THE THIRD PERSON SINGULAR.

SUPERO supero, superare, superavi, superatum

> *present* superat
>
> *future* superabit
>
> *imperfect* superabat
>
> *perfect* superavit

C) TRANSLATE EACH PHRASE INTO LATIN; BE CAREFUL TO CHOOSE THE CORRECT CASE TO FOLLOW *IN.*

1. in the sea   in mari

2. on the animal   in animali

3. on the mound   in tumulo

4. into the town   in oppidum

5. into a window   in fenestram

6. in the region   in regione

D) GIVE THE DEFINITION OF EACH ENGLISH WORD ON THE LINE AND THE LATIN WORD FROM WHICH IT IS DERIVED IN THE PARENTHESES.

1. nepotism   favoritism shown by persons in office to relatives or close friends   (nepos)

2. juvenile   young, characteristic of young   (iuvenis)

3. peninsula   a long projection of land into water   (paene)(insula)

4. tumulus   an ancient grave mound   (tumulus)

E) TRANSLATE THESE SENTENCES.

1. Epulae mensam longam compleverunt. The feast filled the long table.

2. Legio prima in silva errabat. The first legion was wandering in the forest.

3. Pedes et eques in vallo steterunt. A footsoldier and a horseman stood on the wall.

4. Iuvenis in saepem paene erravit. The young person almost wandered into the fence.

5. God created the animals of the land and the fish of the sea and the birds of the sky. Deus animalia terrae et pisces maris et aves caeli creavit.

LESSON 64

A) COMPLETE THIS CHANT.

I lead	duco	ducimus	we lead
you lead	ducis	ducitis	you (all) lead
he, she, it leads	ducit	ducunt	they lead

The chant that you have written is DUCO in the present tense. With that in mind, give the translations on the left and right sides of the chant.

DUCO is an example of a 3rd conjugation verb. If you have not memorized this chant yet, do it now. A 3rd conjugation verb has an infinitive that ends in *ere*. The infinitive of a 2nd conjugation verb ends in *ere*.

What are the other verbs in this week's list that are in the 3rd conjugation?
mitto, frango, vinco, emo

CHOOSE THREE OF THE OTHER 3RD CONJUGATION VERBS AND CONJUGATE THEM ON THE LINES.

mitto	mittimus	emo	emimus	vinco	vincimus
mittis	mittitis	emis	emitis	vincis	vincitis
mittit	mittunt	emit	emunt	vincit	vincunt

B) THE FUTURE TENSE OF THE 3RD CONJUGATION IS QUITE DIFFERENT FROM THE FUTURE TENSE IN THE 1ST AND 2ND CONJUGATIONS. STUDY THE EXAMPLE OF DUCO AND THEN CONJUGATE THE OTHER VERBS IN THE SAME WAY.

ducam	ducemus	emam	ememus
duces	ducetis	emes	emetis
ducet	ducent	emet	ement

vincam	vincemus
vinces	vincetis
vincet	vincent

C) MITTO HAS MANY ENGLISH DERIVATIVES. BY LOOKING AT THE PRINCIPAL PARTS, SEE HOW MANY YOU CAN THINK OF.

transmit, omit, remit, submit, emit, admit, commit, mission, missionary, missile, missive

LESSON 65

A) DECLINE THESE NOUNS ON THE LINES ACCORDING TO THEIR DECLENSIONS. *DIES* IS IN THE 5TH DECLENSION, WHICH YOU HAVE NOT YET HAD, BUT IT FOLLOWS THE ES, EI CHANT, SO SEE IF YOU CAN DO IT. ALTHOUGH THREE OF THESE NOUNS ARE IN THE 3RD DECLENSION, THEY ARE ALL DIFFERENT VARIETIES, SO BE CAREFUL!

vesper	veperes	nox	noctes
vesperis	vesperum	noctis	noctium
vesperi	vesperibus	nocti	noctibus
vesperem	vesperes	noctem	noctes
vespere	vesperibus	nocte	noctibus
tempus	tempora	dies	dies
temporis	temporum	diei	dierum
tempori	temporibus	diei	diebus
tempus	tempora	diem	dies
tempore	temporibus	die	diebus

B) *SCRIBO* IS A 3RD CONJUGATION VERB THAT YOU LEARNED IN THE FIRST BOOK. CONJUGATE IT IN THE PRESENT AND FUTURE TENSES ON THE LINES.

scribo	scribimus	scribam	scribemus
scribis	scribitis	scribes	scribetis
scribit	scribunt	scribet	scribent

C) THE IMPERFECT AND PERFECT TENSES OF THE 3RD CONJUGATION ARE FORMED IN THE SAME WAY AS THEY ARE IN THE 1ST AND 2ND CONJUGATIONS.

For the imperfect tense take the present stem and add the endings *bam, bas, bat...*

ducebam	ducebamus	mittebam	mittebamus
ducebas	ducebatis	mittebas	mittebatis
ducebat	ducebant	mittebat	mittebant

For the perfect tense add *i*, *isti*, *it*... to the perfect stem.

duxi	duximus	misi	misimus
duxisti	duxistis	misisti	misistis
duxit	duxerunt	misit	miserunt

D) TRANSLATE THESE SENTENCES.

1. Saxum rotam franget. The rock will break the wheel.

2. Famulus cibum emit. The male servant buys the food.

3. Senex litteras scribit. The old man is writing a letter.

4. Iuvenes animalia ducunt. The young people are leading the animals.

5. Pastores oves ducent. The shepherds will lead the sheep.

6. Mercatores pecuniam mittent. The merchants will send money.

7. The storm smashed the raft. Tempestas ratem fregit.

8. We will defeat the cavalry. Equites vincemus.

9. The scout will guide the settlers across the region. Explorator incolas trans regionem ducet.

LESSON 66

A) ANOTHER USE FOR THE ABLATIVE CASE IS TO SHOW THE TIME WHEN SOMETHING HAPPENS. IN ENGLISH THIS IS DONE WITH PREPOSITIONAL PHRASES SUCH AS "IN THE NIGHT," "DURING THE FIRST YEAR," AND "AT NOON." IN LATIN, THE TIME CAN SIMPLY BE PUT IN THE ABLATIVE CASE. BELOW ARE SOME EXAMPLES WITH POSSIBLE TRANSLATIONS.

nocte	in the night, during the night
vespere	in the evening, during the evening
anno belli	within the year of the war
Anno Domini	in the year of our Lord

B) TRANSLATE THESE SENTENCES.

1. Erat fames in patria annis belli. <u>There was a famine in the native land in the year of the war.</u>

2. Montes longinquos et mare prima luce viderunt. <u>They saw the distant mountains and sea at dawn.</u>

3. Latrones aedificium per fenestram nocte intraverunt. <u>The robbers entered the building through the window at night.</u>

4. Viri fidi hostes die proeli vicerunt. <u>The faithful men conquered the enemy on the day of battle.</u>

5. They will buy grain during the summer. <u>Frumentum aestate ement.</u>

C) GIVE A SYNOPSIS OF *FRANGO* IN THE 1ST PERSON SINGULAR.

FRANGO <u>frango, frangere, fregi, fractum</u>

      present <u>frango</u>

      future <u>frangam</u>

      imperfect <u>frangebam</u>

      perfect <u>fregi</u>

LESSON 67

A) USE THE LINES BELOW TO CONJUGATE AND COMPARE THESE VERBS IN THE 1ST, 2ND, AND 3RD CONJUGATIONS.

PRESENT

1ST		2ND		3RD	
amo	amamus	video	videmus	duco	ducimus
amas	amatis	vides	videtis	ducis	ducitis
amat	amant	videt	vident	ducit	ducunt

IMPERFECT

1ST		2ND	
amabam	amabamus	videbam	videbamus
amabas	amabatis	videbas	videbatis
amabat	amabant	videbat	videbant

3RD

ducebam	ducebamus
ducebas	ducebatis
ducebat	ducebant

FUTURE

amabo	amabimus	videbo	videbimus
amabis	amabitis	videbis	videbitis
amabit	amabunt	videbit	videbunt

ducam	ducemus
duces	ducetis
ducet	ducent

PERFECT

amavi	amavimus	vidi	vidimus
amavisti	amavistis	vidisti	vidistis
amavit	amaverunt	vidit	viderunt

	duxi	duximus	
	duxisti	duxistis	
	duxit	duxerunt	

B) TRANSLATE THESE SENTENCES.

1. Agricola animalia in stabulum misit. <u>The farmer sent the animals into the stable.</u>

2. Puer boves trans vallem vocavit. <u>The boy called the cows across the valley.</u>

3. Femina liberos per fenestram vidit. <u>The woman saw the children through the window.</u>

4. The sheep were lying on the hills. <u>Oves in tumulis (collibus) iacebant.</u>

C) IN LESSON 59 THERE WERE SOME COMPOUND WORDS FORMED FROM *STO*. *PRAESTO* IS ANOTHER COMPOUND WORD FORMED FROM *STO*. IT MEANS "TO STAND BEFORE, EXCEL, BE OUTSTANDING." BELOW ARE THREE COMPOUNDS MADE BY ADDING THE PREFIX *PRAE* TO OTHER BASE WORDS. BY CONSIDERING THE BASE WORDS, DECIDE WHICH DEFINITION BELONGS WITH WHICH WORD.

DEFINITIONS: send ahead

be in charge of something

place someone in charge of something

praeficio	place someone in charge of something
praemitto	send ahead
praesum	be in charge of something

LESSON 68

A) CREDO, REGO, PONO, CURRO, SERO, AND DIRIGO ARE 3RD CONJUGATION VERBS
THAT YOU LEARNED IN THE FIRST YEAR OF LATIN. CHOOSE ONE OF THESE AND WRITE
ITS PRINCIPAL PARTS ON THE LINE AND THEN CONJUGATE IT ON THE LINES.

PRINCIPAL PARTS pono, ponere, posui, positum

PRESENT		FUTURE	
pono	ponimus	ponam	ponemus
ponis	ponitis	pones	ponetis
ponit	ponunt	ponet	ponent

IMPERFECT		PERFECT	
ponebam	ponebamus	posui	posuimus
ponebas	ponebatis	posuisti	posuistis
ponebat	ponebant	posuit	posuerunt

B) DECLINE MARE AND ANIMAL FROM MEMORY ON THE LINES.

mare	maria	animal	animalia
maris	marium	animalis	animalium
mari	maribus	animali	animalibus
mare	maria	animal	animalia
mari	maribus	animali	animalibus

C) TRANSLATE THESE SENTENCES.

1. Iuvenis onus ligni in aedificium portabat. The young person was carrying the load of wood into the building.

2. Dux nuntios quattuor trans regionem misit simul. <u>The general sent four messengers across the region at the same time.</u>

3. Fax nunti ardebat nocte. <u>The messenger's torch was burning during the night.</u>

4. Nuntius facem epistulamque comiti dedit. <u>The messenger gave the torch and the letter to the associate.</u>

5. Vesper nuntium citum per tenebras duxit. <u>The evening star led the swift messenger through the darkness.</u>

6. Dux nuntium in via vidit. <u>The general saw the messenger on the road.</u>

D) WHAT ARE THE TWO USES FOR THE ABLATIVE CASE THAT YOU HAVE LEARNED?

1. <u>place where</u>

2. <u>time when</u>

LESSON 69

A) DECLINE THE SINGULAR FORMS OF *HIC* ON THE LINES AND TRANSLATE IN THE PARENTHESES.

MASCULINE		FEMININE		NEUTER	
hic	(this man)	haec	(this woman)	hoc	(this thing)
huius	(of)	huius	(____)	huius	(____)
huic	(to, for this)	huic	(____)	huic	(____)
hunc	(this)	hanc	(____)	hoc	(____)
hoc	(by, with, from, this)	hac	(____)	hoc	(____)

DECLINE THE PLURAL FORMS IN THE BOXES AND TRANSLATE.

hi	(these men)	hae	(these women)	haec	(these things)
horum	(of these)	harum	(____)	horum	(____)
his	(to, for these)	his	(____)	his	(____)
hos	(these)	has	(____)	haec	(____)
his	(by these)	his	(____)	his	(____)

Hic and all its forms can be used as a pronoun, taking the place of a noun, or as an adjective, modifying a noun. When it is used as an adjective, it needs to match the noun it modifies in <u>gender</u>, <u>number</u>, and <u>case</u>.

B) TRANSLATE THESE SENTENCES AND IDENTIFY WHETHER THE FORM OF *HIC* IS USED AS AN PRONOUN OR AN ADJECTIVE.

                              adj.
1. Hic cibus est bonus. <u>This food is good.</u>

2. Incolae harum urbium classem servaverunt. adj. <u>The inhabitants of these cities saved the fleet.</u>

pron.
3. Haec est meta. <u>This is the goal.</u>

pron.
4. Hi sunt liberi ludi. <u>These are the children of the school.</u>

adj.
5. Hae aves sunt pulchrae. <u>These birds are beautiful.</u>

LESSON 70

A) TRANSLATE THESE SENTENCES. UNDERLINE ANY WORDS YOU NEED TO LOOK UP.

1. Fumus densus ignis montes occultavit. The dense smoke of the fire hid the mountains.

2. Arbores silvae ardebant. The trees of the forest were burning.

3. Copiae ferae ad urbes campi appropinquaverunt. The fierce troops approached the cities of the plain.

4. Liberi beneficium matris semper commemorabunt. The children will always remember the kindness of the mother.

5. Nuntius litteras trans hanc regionem asperam portabat. The messenger was carrying the letter across this harsh region.

6. Litteras duci salve dedit. He gave the letter safely to the leader.

7. Potestne frangere vir marmorem? Is the man able to break the marble?

8. Adulescens marmorem paene fregit. The young man almost broke the marble.

B) TRANSLATE THESE PHRASES INTO LATIN, USING THE NOMINATIVE CASE.

1. this herd	hoc armentum, hic grex
2. these sheep	haec ovis
3. these swift horses	hi citi equi
4. these steep hills	hi colles ardui
5. this building	hoc aedificium
6. this beautiful and quiet island	haec insula pulchra et quieta

LESSON 71

A) GIVE A SYNOPSIS OF *DO* IN THE 1ST PERSON PLURAL.

DO <u>do, dare, dedi, datum</u>

present	<u>damus</u>	<u>we give</u>
future	<u>dabimus</u>	<u>we shall give</u>
imperfect	<u>dabamus</u>	<u>we were giving</u>
perfect	<u>dedimus</u>	<u>we gave</u>

B) CHECK YOUR KNOWLEDGE OF THIS VOCABULARY BY TRANSLATING EACH WORD. CIRCLE ANY THAT YOU CANNOT DO BY MEMORY.

1. culmen	<u>top, peak, high point</u>	9. reus	<u>defendant</u>
2. palus	<u>swamp</u>	10. epulae	<u>feast</u>
3. litus	<u>shore</u>	11. torreo	<u>burn, parch, roast</u>
4. periculum	<u>danger</u>	12. avaritia	<u>greed</u>
5. hospes	<u>guest, host</u>	13. argentum	<u>silver</u>
6. benevolentia	<u>kindness, good-will</u>	14. culpa	<u>fault, blame</u>
7. iudex	<u>judge, juror</u>	15. hoc	<u>this</u>
8. concilio	<u>win, win over</u>	16. horum	<u>of these</u>

C. TRANSLATE THESE SENTENCES.

1. Regis epulae mensam longam compleverunt. <u>The king's feast filled the long table.</u>

2. Onus magnum mensam firmam non franget. <u>The great burden will not break the sturdy table</u>.

3. Nautae periti per angustias hieme navigaverunt. <u>The skilled sailors sailed through the narrows in winter</u>.

4. Dux et milites quinque in vallo stabant. <u>The general and five soldiers were standing on the wall</u>.

5. Explorator faces in culmine scopuli celsi potest videre. <u>The scout is able to see torches on the top of the high cliff</u>.

D) Circle the correct meanings of these English words based on your knowledge of their Latin sources.

1. A *vestige* is a

    a) small entrance hall

    (b) trace of something that has now passed away

    c) a long, flat sled

2. To be *culpable* is to

    a) be visible

    b) be capable

    (c) deserve blame

3. *Benevolence* is a

    a) tendency to anger quickly

    b) suspicious nature

    (c) desire to do good

LESSON 72

A) TRANSLATE AND ANALYZE EACH SENTENCE. (FOR NOUNS GIVE FUNCTION, CASE, AND NUMBER, FOR VERBS GIVE TENSE AND PRONOUN.)

1. Nautae defessi litora patriae vident. <u>The weary sailors see the shores of the native land.</u> NAUTAE—subject, nominative, plural; LITORA—direct object, accusative, plural; PATRIAE—possession, genitive, singular; VIDENT—present, they

2. Rotae carri sunt novae. <u>The wheels of the wagon are new.</u> ROTAE—subject, nom., plural; CARRI—possession, gen., singular; SUNT—present, they

3. Coniunx coniugi laetae flores dedit. <u>The husband gave flowers to the happy wife.</u> CONIUNX—subject, nom., singular; CONIUGI—indirect object, dat., singular; FLORES—direct object, acc., plural; DEDIT—perfect, he

4. Navis longa cibum trans mare portabat. <u>The long ship (man of war) was carrying food across the sea.</u> NAVIS—subject, nom., singular; CIBUM—direct object, acc., singular; MARE—object of prep. trans, acc., singular; PORTABAT—imperfect, it

5. Armentum cervorum in lucum nocte movebit. <u>The herd of deer will move into the grove at night</u>. ARMENTUM—subject, nom., singular; CERVORUM—genitive of material (This term has not been used, although there have been sentences with it in them.) plural; LUCUM—object of prep. in, acc., singular; NOCTE—time when, abl., singular; MOVEBIT—future, it

6. Pater materque filios filiasque benevolentiam et misericordiam docuerunt. <u>Father and mother taught sons and daughters kindness and mercy.</u> PATER, MATER—sub., nom., sing.; FILIOS, FILIAS—acc. of person taught with doceo, plural; BENEVOLENTIAM, MISERICORDIAM—acc. of thing taught with doceo, singular; DOCUERUNT—perfect, they

LESSON 73

A) ABOVE EACH CHANT, WRITE THE NOMINATIVE AND GENITIVE FORMS, GENDER, AND MEANING OF THE GIVEN NOUN, THEN DECLINE IT ON THE LINES.

META, METAE F. TURNING POINT

meta	metae
metae	metarum
metae	metis
metam	metas
meta	metis

LUCUS, LUCI M. GROVE

lucus	luci
luci	lucorum
luco	lucis
lucum	lucos
luco	lucis

VALLUM, VALLI N. RAMPART, WALL

vallum	valla
valli	vallorum
vallo	vallis
vallum	valla
vallo	vallis

CINIS, CINERIS M. ASHES

cinis	cineres
cineris	cinerum
cineri	cineribus
cinerem	cineres
cinere	cineribus

FULMEN, FULMINIS N. THUNDERBOLT, LIGHTNING

fulmen	fulmina
fulminis	fulminum
fulmini	fulminibus
fulmen	fulmina
fulmine	fulminibus

RATIS, RATIS F. RAFT, BOAT

ratis	rates
ratis	ratium
rati	ratibus
ratem	rates
rate	ratibus

FONS, FONTIS M. SPRING

fons	fontes
fontis	fontium
fonti	fontibus
fontem	fontes
fonte	fontibus

MARE, MARIS N. SEA

mare	maria
maris	marium
mari	maribus
mare	maria
mari	maribus

B) Give the reason (the declension and special category within a declension) for declining each of the nouns above as you did.

	DECLENSION	CATEGORY
1. meta	1st declension	feminine
2. lucus	2nd declension	masculine
3. vallum	2nd declension	neuter
4. cinis	3rd declension	masculine
5. fulmen	3rd declension	neuter
6. ratis	3rd declension	feminine i-stem—same number of syllables in nom. and gen., and endings are is, is or es is
7. fons	3rd declension	masculine i-stem—nom. form ends in "s" or "x" and base end in 2 consonants
8. mare	3rd declension	neuter i-stem—neuter that ends in e, al, or ar.

C) Translate these sentences into Latin.

1. The children liked the wild games, but the mothers liked the quiet games. Liberi ludos feros amaverunt, sed matres ludos quietos amaverunt.

2. The birds of the forest were singing at dawn. Aves silvae prima luce cantabant.

3. They walked happily on the road and saw many flowers in the fields. In via laete ambulaverunt et flores multas in agris viserunt.

LESSON 74

A) CONJUGATE AND COMPARE THESE VERBS IN THE 1ST, 2ND, AND 3RD CONJUGATIONS.

PRESENT

1ST		2ND		3RD	
sono	sonamus	luceo	lucemus	emo	emimus
sonas	sonatis	luces	lucetis	emis	emitis
sonat	sonant	lucet	lucent	emit	emunt

IMPERFECT

1ST		2ND	
sonabam	sonabamus	lucebam	lucebamus
sonabas	sonabatis	lucebas	lucebatis
sonabat	sonabant	lucebat	lucebant

3RD

emebam	emebamus
emebas	emebatis
emebat	emebant

FUTURE

sonabo	sonabimus	lucebo	lucebimus
sonabis	sonabitis	lucebis	lucebitis
sonabit	sonabunt	lucebit	lucebunt

emam	ememus
emes	emetis
emet	ement

PERFECT

<u>sonavi</u>	<u>sonavimus</u>	<u>luxi</u>	<u>luximus</u>
<u>sonavisti</u>	<u>sonavistis</u>	<u>luxisti</u>	<u>luxistis</u>
<u>sonavit</u>	<u>sonaverunt</u>	<u>luxit</u>	<u>luxerunt</u>

<u>emi</u>	<u>emimus</u>
<u>emisti</u>	<u>emistis</u>
<u>emit</u>	<u>emerunt</u>

B) TRANSLATE THESE SENTENCES.

1. Tempestas per vallem sonavit et fulmen in caelo canduit. <u>The storm resounded through the valley and lightning was white in the sky.</u>

2. Flammae gramen *siccum campi aestate torruerunt sed gramen umidum vallis non torruerunt. <u>Flames burned the dry grass of the plain during summer but did not burn the wet grass of the valley.</u>

3. Iuvenis vestigia in harena vidit. <u>The young person saw footprints on the beach.</u>

4. Vestigia iuvenem in antrum obscurum duxerunt. <u>The footprints led the young person into a hidden cave.</u>

5. Fratres Iosephi frumentum tempore famis emerunt. <u>The brothers of Joseph bought grain in the time of the famine.</u>

*You haven't had this word on a list but use your dictionary to figure it out.

C) Translate these sentences into Latin. Remember how these verbs are used.

1. The good food pleased the sick man. <u>Cibus bonus viro aegro placuit.</u>

2. The master entrusted the money to the slave. <u>Dominus pecuniam servo mandavit.</u>

3. The farmer put a fence around the horses. <u>Agricola saepem equis circumedit.</u>

4. The father taught the sons the dangers of the swamp. <u>Pater filios pericula paludis docuit.</u>

CARMEN POSSUM

The nox was lit by lux of Luna,
And 'twas a nox most opportuna
To catch a possum or a coona;
For nix was scattered o'er this mundus,
A shallow nix, et non profundus.
On sic a nox with canis unus,
Two boys went out to hunt for coonus.
The corpus of this bonus canis
Was full as long as octo span is,
But brevior legs had canis never
Quam had hic dog; et bonus clever,
Some used to say, in stultum jocum
Quod a field was too small locum
For sic a dog to make a turnus
Circum self from stem to sternus.
Unus canis, duo puer,
Nunquam braver, nunquam truer,
Quam hoc trio nunquam fuit,
If there was I never knew it.
This bonus dog had one bad habit,
Amabat much to tree a rabbit,
Amabat plus to chase a rattus,
Amabat bene tree a cattus.
But on this nixy moonlight night
This old canis did just right.
Nunquam treed a starving rattus,
Nunquam chased a starving cattus.
But sucurrit on, intentus
On the track and on the scentus,

Till he trees a possum strongum,
In a hollow trunkum longum.
Loud he barked in horrid bellum,
Seemed on terra vehit pellum.
Quickly ran the duo puer
Mors of possum to secure.
Quam venerit, one began
To chop away like quisque man.
Soon the axe went through the truncum
Soon he hit it all kerchunkum;
Combat deepens, on ye braves!
Canis, pueri, et staves;
As his powers non longius tarry,
Possum potest, non pugnare.
On the nix his corpus lieth.
Down to Hades spirit flieth,
Joyful pueri, canis bonus,
Think him dead as any stonus.
Now they seek their pater's domo,
Feeling proud as any homo,
Knowing, certe, they will blossom
Into heroes, when with possum
They arrive, narrabunt story,
Plenus blood et plenior glory.
Pompey, David, Samson, Caesar,
Cyrus, Black Hawk, Shalmanezer!
Tell me where est now the gloria,
Where the honors of victoria?
Nunc a domum narrent story,
Plenus sanguine, tragic, gory.
Pater praiseth, likewise mater,
Wonders greatly younger frater.

Possum leave they on the mundus,
Go themselves to sleep profundus,
Somniunt possums slain in battle,
Strong as ursae, large as cattle.
When nox gives way to lux of morning,
Albam terram much adorning,
Up they jump to see the varmen,
Of the which this is the carmen.
Lo! possum est resurrectum!
Ecce pueri dejectum,
Ne relinquit track behind him,
Et the pueri never find him.
Cruel possum! bestia vilest,
How the pueros thou beguilest!
Pueri think non plus of Caesar,
Nor of Samson, Shalmanezer,
Take your laurels, cum the honor,
Since ista possum is a goner!

CHANT SUMMARIES

VERBS

ACTIVE VOICE

PRESENT		FUTURE		IMPERFECT	
o	mus	bo	bimus	bam	bamus
s	tis	bis	bitis	bas	batis
t	nt	bit	bunt	bat	bant

PERFECT		FUTURE PERFECT		PLUPERFECT	
i	imus	ero	erimus	eram	eramus
isti	istis	eris	eritis	eras	eratis
it	erunt	erit	erint	erat	erant

EXAMPLES IN THE PRESENT TENSE:

FIRST CONJUGATION		SECOND CONJUGATION		THIRD CONJUGATION		FOURTH CONJUGATION	
amo	amamus	video	videmus	duco	ducimus	audio	audimus
amas	amatis	vides	videtis	ducis	ducitis	audis	auditis
amat	amant	videt	vident	ducit	ducunt	audit	audiunt

PASSIVE VOICE

PASSIVE PRESENT		PASSIVE FUTURE		PASSIVE IMPERFECT	
r	mur	bor	bimur	bar	bamur
ris	mini	beris	bimini	baris	bamini
tur	ntur	bitur	buntur	batur	bantur

THE BEING VERB

PRESENT INDICATIVE, "I AM"		PRESENT INDICATIVE, "I AM ABLE"	
sum	sumus	possum	possumus
es	estis	potes	potestis
est	sunt	potest	possunt

NOUNS

FIRST DECLENSION		SECOND DECL. (M & F)		SECOND DECL. (N)		THIRD DECL. (M & F)	
a	ae	us	i	um	a	x	es
ae	arum	i	orum	i	orum	is	um
ae	is	o	is	o	is	i	ibus
am	as	um	os	um	a	em	es
a	is	o	is	o	is	e	ibus

THIRD DECL. (N)		FOURTH DECL. (M & F)		FOURTH DECL. (N)		FIFTH DECLENSION	
x	es	us	us	u	ua	es	es
is	um	us	uum	us	uum	ei	erum
i	ibus	ui	ibus	u	ibus	ei	ebus
x	es	um	us	u	ua	em	es
e	ibus	u	ibus	u	ibus	e	ebus

DEMONSTRATIVES

"THIS," SINGULAR

hic	haec	hoc
huius	huius	huius
huic	huic	huic
hunc	hanc	hoc
hoc	hac	hoc

"THIS," PLURAL

hi	hae	haec
horum	harum	horum
his	his	his
hos	has	haec
his	his	his

"THAT," SINGULAR

ille	illa	illud
illius	illius	illius
illi	illi	illi
illum	illam	illud
illo	illa	illo

"THAT," PLURAL

illi	illae	illa
illorum	illarum	illorum
illis	illis	illis
illos	illas	illa
illis	illis	illis

PERSONAL PRONOUNS

FIRST & SECOND PERSON

SING. (I)	SING. (YOU)	PL. (WE)	PL. (YOU)
ego	tu	nos	vos
mei	tui	nostrum	vestrum
mihi	tibi	nobis	vobis
me	te	nos	vos
me	te	nobis	vobis

THIRD PERSON

SINGULAR M	F	N	PLURAL M	F	N
is	ea	id	ei	eae	ea
eius	eius	eius	eorum	earum	eorum
ei	ei	ei	eis	eis	eis
eum	eam	id	eos	eas	ea
eo	ea	eo	eis	eis	eis

RELATIVE PRONOUNS

SINGULAR M	F	N	PLURAL M	F	N
qui	quae	quod	qui	quae	quae
cuius	cuius	cuius	quorum	quarum	quorum
cui	cui	cui	quibus	quibus	quibus
quem	quam	quod	quos	quas	quae
quo	qua	quo	quibus	quibus	quibus

TRANSLATIONS

UNIT 4

1. Mercator acutus argentum conservabat.

2. Reus laetus ridet.

3. Exploratores regionem quietam spectant.

4. Virgo trepida serpentem vitabit.

5. Incolae oppidum parant.

6. Latrones mali aedificium spectabant.

7. Latro malus ad fenestram appropinquat.

8. Videtne custos defessus latronem?

9. Canis ferus et magnus latrones malos terrebit.

10. Iudices sententiam mutabunt.

11. Erimusne victores?

12. Dux socium peritum et fidum rogabat.

13. Conciliabimus proelium ferum.

14. Humus umidus proelium tardabit.

15. Eratis magni heroes.

16. Novi et ignari incolae erant .

17. Famulus trepidum ad dominum severum appropinquabat.

18. Silvae densae et montes alti et harenae bellae exploratores delectabant.

KEY

1. The intelligent merchant was saving money.

2. The happy defendant smiles.

3. The explorers are looking at the quiet region.

4. The trembling maiden will avoid the snake.

5. The inhabitants are preparing the town.

6. Evil robbers were watching the building.

7. The evil robber is drawing near to the window.

8. Does the weary watchman see the robber?

9. The fierce large dog will frighten the evil robbers.

10. The jurors will change the decision.

11. Shall we be victors?

12. The general was asking the skilled and faithful ally.

13. We shall win the fierce battle.

14. Wet ground will delay the battle.

15. You (all) were great heroes.

16. They were new and ignorant settlers.

17. The trembling servant was approaching the strict master.

18. The dense forests and high mountains and pretty beaches were delighting the explorers.

Unit 5

1. Duo pueri ratem portabant.

2. Poena erit severa.

3. Mater vestem pulchram filiae parat.

4. Famula hortum magnum domino parabat.

5. Dux et socii ad provinciam appropinquabunt.

6. Puer libros bonos fratri dabit.

7. Deus vivus vitam hominibus dat.

8. Comes fidus erat amicus verus.

9. Adulescens contentus piscem magnum portabat.

10. Pater ludos novos filios docebat.

Key

1. Two boys were carrying the raft.

2. The penalty will be severe.

3. The mother is preparing the beautiful garment for the daughter.

4. The servant was preparing the large garden for the master.

5. The leader and the associates will approach the province.

6. The boy will give the good books to the brother.

7. The living God gives life to men.

8. The faithful companion was a true friend.

9. The satisfied young man was carrying a large fish.

10. The father was teaching new games to the sons.

Unit 6

1. Rex coronam filio dabit.

2. Praedo avem socio mandabit.

3. Roma est urbs antiqua.

4. Pastor gregem canibus mandat.

5. Tempestates et montes et viri improbi heroem tardant sed superabit.

6. Puella margaritas stulte iecit pro porcis.

7. Navis ad litus latum salve appropinquat.

8. Proelium ferum legatum aegrum perturbabat.

9. Rex potens leges bonas populo dat.

10. Femina flores graminibus cras circumdabit.

Key

1. The king will give the crown to the son.

2. The pirate will entrust the bird to the ally.

3. Rome is an ancient city.

4. The shepherd entrusts the flock to the dogs.

5. Storms and mountains and wicked men are delaying the hero, but he will overcome.

6. The girl foolishly threw the pearls before the pigs.

7. The ship is safely approaching the wide shore.

8. The fierce battle was confusing the sick lieutenant.

9. The powerful king gives good laws to the people.

10. The woman will put flowers around the grass tomorrow.

UNIT 7

1. Dentes leonis pastorem non terrebant.

2. Vultus hospitis erat gratus.

3. Fons parvus est gelidus.

4. Gurgites fluminis erant obscuri.

5. Sol erat obscurus heri.

6. Dux novus milites peritos conciliabit.

7. Flammae gramen regionis torrent.

8. Naves praedonum appropinquabant ad harenas insulae.

9. Agricola saepem ovibus circumdabit cras.

10. Famuli fidi domino bono placent.

KEY

1. The lion's teeth were not frightening the shepherd.

2. The face of the guest was grateful.

3. The little spring is cold.

4. The whirlpools of the river were hidden.

5. The sun was hidden yesterday.

6. The new general will win over the experienced soldiers.

7. Flames are burning the grass of the region.

8. The pirates' ships were approaching the beaches of the island.

9. The farmer will put a fence around the sheep tomorrow.

10. The faithful servants please the good master.

UNIT 8

1. Litus est longinquum et quietum.

2. Equi sunt citi pulchrique.

3. Agricola frumenta bona habet trans vallem.

4. Explorator in paludem obscuram ambulabit.

5. Scopulus arduus erat meta itineris.

6. Avis praedonis carmina cantabat.

7. Leo pastorem vulnervit per vestem.

8. Vir equum per flumen ursit.

9. Nimbi nigri frumentum album impendebant.

10. Constantia et virtus pastoris canisque servaverunt gregem ovium.

KEY

1. The shore is distant and quiet.

2. Horses are swift and beautiful.

3. The farmer has good crops across the valley.

4. The explorer will walk into the hidden swamp.

5. The steep cliff was the goal of the journey.

6. The pirate's bird was singing songs.

7. A lion wounded the shepherd through the garment.

8. The man urged the horse through the river.

9. Black clouds were threatening the white grain.

10. The constancy and courage of the shepherd and the dog saved the flock of sheep.

UNIT 9

1. Mare erat gelidum.

2. Pastor gregem per tenebras ursit.

3. Sententia iudicis fuit iusta.

4. Mercator vestes pulchras emet in urbe.

5. Virgae arborum in via iter incolarum tardabant.

6. Senex lacum et lucum laurorum per fenestram potest videre.

7. Incolae frumenta in agris heri severunt.

8. Deus misericordiam benevolentiamque hominibus monstrat.

9. Tempestates multae hieme lacum compleverunt.

10. Avus nepoti caro fabulas miras aestate recitavit.

KEY

1. The sea was cold.

2. The shepherd urged the flock through the darkness.

3. The opinion of the juror was just.

4. The merchant will buy beautiful clothing in the city.

5. Branches of trees in the road were delaying the journey of the settlers.

6. The old man is able to see the lake and the grove of laurel trees through the window.

7. The settlers planted crops in the fields yesterday.

8. God shows mercy and good will to men.

9. The many storms filled up the lake during the winter.

10. The grandfather read aloud wonderful stories to the dear grandson during the summer.

Unit 10

1. Hic carrus rotas magnas non habet.

2. Ignis magnus tecta urbis delebat.

3. Scopuli montis erant ardui.

4. Antrum obscurum adulescentem parvum terruit.

5. Naves classis gurgitem salve vitaverunt.

6. Sagitarius peritus vestigia leonis trans vallem videt.

7. Silva magna erit latebra praedonum malorum.

8. Divitiae huius viri curam augebunt.

9. Carmina pulchra auribus bovis non placent.

10. Hic fidus famulus est carus agricolae.

Key

1. This wagon does not have large wheels.

2. A great fire was destroying the dwellings of the city.

3. The cliffs of the mountain were steep.

4. The dark cave frightened the small young man.

5. The ships of the fleet safely avoided the whirlpool.

6. The skillful archer sees the tracks of the lion across the valley.

7. The great forest will be the hiding place of the evil pirates.

8. The riches of this man will increase care.

9. The beautiful songs are not pleasing to the ears of the cow.

10. This faithful servant is dear to the farmer.

TEST BLANKS

TEST 1

A) GIVE THE ENGLISH TRANSLATION FOR THESE WORDS AND LABEL THEM ACCORDING TO WHETHER THEY ARE NOUNS (N) OR ADJECTIVES (A).

_____ campus _____   _____ umidus _____

_____ heros _____   _____ argentum _____

_____ fenestra _____

B) TRANSLATE THESE VERBS.

1. Ridebo.   _____

2. Portas.   _____

3. Lucet.   _____

4. Tardabis.   _____

5. Amabunt.   _____

6. Ridebimus.   _____

7. Portamus.   _____

8. Tardo.   _____

9. Lucent.   _____

10. Amabit.   _____

C) COMPLETE EACH STATEMENT BY WRITING "NOUNS," "VERBS," OR "ADJECTIVES" IN THE BLANK.

1. *o, s, t, mus, tis* and *nt* are endings for Latin _____.

2. _____ name a person, place, or thing.

3. Most Latin _____ have three endings so they can match the noun they are describing.

4. _____ express action or state of being.

5. The endings on Latin _____ tell whether it is singular or plural and what its function is in the sentence.

D) LIST FIVE DERIVATIVES AND THE LATIN WORD EACH CAME FROM.

1. _____

2. _____

3. _____

4. _____

5. _____

Name: _____

Date: _____

TEST 2

A) FILL IN THE BLANKS.

The accusative singular ending in the 1st declension is_____.

In the 2nd declension it is_____ and in the 3rd it is_____.

The accusative plural ending in the 1st declension is_____.

In the 2nd declension it is _____ and in the 3rd it is____.

B) GIVE THE TRANSLATION AND ACCUSATIVE SINGULAR FORM OF THESE NOUNS IN LATIN.

	TRANSLATION	ACCUSATIVE SING. FORM
1. harena	_____	_____
2. astrum	_____	_____
3. lapis	_____	_____
4. ratis	_____	_____
5. lucus	_____	_____

C) TRANSLATE THESE. (CAREFULLY)

1. Pecunia incolam delectat. _____

2. Incolae montem explorabunt. _____

3. Avaritia est culpa. _____

4. Ventus ratem agitat. _____

5. Fulmen candet. _____

6. Nauta rates convocabit. _____

7. The smoke frightens the horse. _____

8. The groves are laurel trees. _____

D) WHAT IS THE FUNCTION OF THESE WORDS IN THE SENTENCES ABOVE?

pecunia in #1 _____

montem in #2 _____

avaritia in #3 _____

E) GIVE THE LATIN ORIGIN FOR THESE ENGLISH WORDS:

1. sylvan   _____

2. floriculture   _____

3. lapidary   _____

4. convocation   _____

What element is "au" the chemical symbol for? _____

TEST 3

A) AN ADJECTIVE MODIFIES A _____ OR A _____. IT CAN TELL _____, _____, OR _____.

A Latin adjective matches what it modifies in three ways: _____, _____, and _____.

The three genders are _____, _____, and _____.

B) TRANSLATE THESE PHRASES INTO LATIN, MATCHING EVERYTHING THAT NEEDS TO BE. USE THE NOMINATIVE CASE.

1. new road   _____

2. evil master   _____

3. intelligent watchman   _____

4. cold building   _____

5. faithful male servants   _____

C) TRANSLATE THESE SENTENCES.

1. Caterva rauca aedificium vitat. _____

_____

2. Famuli laeti gregem novum demonstrant. _____

_____

3. Frumenta flammae ferae torrent. _____

_____

4. The intelligent merchant will prepare the way. _____

_____

D) DECLINE THE PHRASE *HORTUS QUIETUS* ON THE LINES BELOW.

_____ _____

_____ _____

_____ _____

_____ _____

_____ _____

What is a "hortus quietus"?_____

TEST 4

A) GIVE THE PRINCIPAL PARTS OF THESE VERBS FROM MEMORY:

amo, _____, _____, _____

rogo, _____, _____, _____

sum, _____, _____, _____

Give the present stem of amo: _____ and rogo: _____

What three tenses is the present stem used for? _____,

_____, _____.

B) TRANSLATE THESE VERBS.

1. conciliare   _____

2. peccabat   _____

3. mutabam   _____

4. conservabant   _____

C) FINISH THE CONJUGATION OF SUM IN THE IMPERFECT TENSE ON THE LINES AND TRANSLATE IT ON THE SIDE.

eram   _____

_____ _____

_____ _____

D) DECLINE *LABOR* ON THE LINES BELOW.

_____   _____

_____   _____

_____   _____

_____   _____

_____   _____

E) TRANSLATE THESE SENTENCES.

1. Navigabuntne exploratores? _____

_____

2. Damnabitne iudex severus latronem? _____

_____

3. Virgo proelium spectat. _____

_____

4. Porta litteras. _____

5. Appropinquate ad ducem. _____

_____

6. The defendant was ignorant. _____

_____

7. The victors were spending the winter. _____

_____

Name: _____

Date: _____

TEST 5

A) GIVE A SYNOPSIS OF CANTO IN THE 2ND PERSON SINGULAR. EXCEPT FOR THE PRINCIPAL PARTS, INCLUDE THE ENGLISH TRANSLATION OF ALL FORMS.

CANTO _____

       present _____

       future _____

       imperfect _____

B) DECLINE THESE 3RD DECLENSION NOUNS.

   vestis   _____   hospes   _____

   _____   _____   _____   _____

   _____   _____   _____   _____

   _____   _____   _____   _____

   _____   _____   _____   _____

C) GIVE THE DATIVE FORMS OF THESE NOUNS.

	SINGULAR	PLURAL
1. turba	_____	_____
2. mater	_____	_____
3. ludus	_____	_____

D) TRANSLATE THESE SENTENCES.

1. Mulier carmen gratum liberos docet. _____

_____

2. Liberi carmina turbae cantabunt. _____

_____

3. Deus misericordiam populo demonstrabat. _____

_____

4. Agricola saepem bovi caro circumdat. _____

_____

5. The father is giving wine to the guest. _____

_____

Test 6

A) Fill in the blanks.

An adjective modifies a _____ or a _____.

An adverb modifies a _____, an _____, or an _____.
It can tell _____, _____, _____, or _____.

An English adverb often has ___ on the end. To form a Latin adverb
from an adjective, ___ is added to the base of the adjective. The base is
found by removing the ending from the _____ form of the adjective.

B) In the first blank write the translation of the Latin word. In the
second blank write whether it is an adjective or an adverb.

1. bene _____ _____

2. praeclarus _____ _____

3. ardua _____ _____

4. praeclare _____ _____

5. firmi _____ _____

C) Form an adverb from these adjectives and then translate the adverb.

1. pulcher, pulchra, pulchrum _____

2. malus, mala, malum _____

D) TRANSLATE THESE SENTENCES.

1. Puer culmina longinqua significabat. _____

_____

2. Dux periculum civibus firme nuntiabit. _____

_____

3. Avis bene cantabat sed canis male cantabat. _____

_____

4. Agricola canem adulescenti mandat. _____

_____

5. Praedones litus scopulosque vident. _____

_____

TEST 7

A) THE GENITIVE CASE IS USED TO SHOW _____. IT CAN BE TRANSLATED WITH THE WORD _____ OR WITH AN _____.

Translate these words in the genitive case:

1. viri _____

2. ovium _____

3. mortis _____

4. pastoris _____

5. leonum _____

B) TRANSLATE THESE SENTENCES.

1. Vir est pastor. _____

2. Insula erit latebra. _____

3. Oves sunt albae. _____

4. Pastor erat asper. _____

The last word in #1 and #2 is a _____.

The last word in #3 and #4 is a _____.

C) TRANSLATE THESE SENTENCES.

1. Vestigium leonis erat magnum. _____

_____

2. Constantia pastoris gregem servat. _____

_____

3. "Ego sum pastor bonus." _____

_____

4. Pastor oves urgebat heri. _____

_____

5. Mors ovium pastorem vexat. _____

_____

6. Oves sunt divitiae pastoris. _____

_____

TEST 8

A) CONJUGATE *ERRO* IN THE PERFECT TENSE AND TRANSLATE IT.

_____   _____

_____   _____

_____   _____

B) CROSS OUT THE INCORRECT TRANSLATION IN EACH SET.

1. postulaverunt

   they were demanding   *they did demand*   *they have demanded*

2. erravisti

   you have wandered   *you will have wandered*   *you wandered*

C) GIVE THE SYNOPSIS AS PRESCRIBED.

STO _____

first person plural

   present _____

   future _____

   imperfect _____

   perfect _____

D) TRANSLATE THESE SENTENCES.

1. Leo in urbem erravit. _____

_____

2. Limen tecti est parvum. _____

_____

3. Legionem primam viri accusaverunt. _____

_____

4. The small fleet wandered through the islands. _____

_____

What case is *tecti* in #2? _____

What case, gender, and number is *legionem* in #3? _____

E) Write three correct translations for this verb.

accusavit _____

_____

F) Translate "Quintili Vare, legiones redde." _____

_____

Who said it? _____

Why? _____

Test 9

A) Conjugate *duco* in the present, future, imperfect, and perfect.

PRESENT   FUTURE

_____ _____   _____ _____

_____ _____   _____ _____

_____ _____   _____ _____

IMPERFECT   PERFECT

_____ _____   _____ _____

_____ _____   _____ _____

_____ _____   _____ _____

B) Translate these phrases and words into Latin.

1. during the night _____   4. at night _____

2. into the sea _____   5. in the year of war_____

3. in the sea _____   6. on the mound _____

C) Translate these sentences.

1. Securis iuvenis lignum fregit. _____

_____

2. Senex nepotes simul vocavit. _____

_____

3. Animal defessum trans limine iacebat. _____

_____

4. Legionem die proelii vincemus. _____

_____

Name: _____

Date: _____

Final Test

A) Give synopses for these verbs as prescribed.

MANDO _____

    third person singular

        present _____

        future _____

        imperfect _____

        perfect _____

URGEO _____

    second person plural

        present _____

        future _____

        imperfect _____

        perfect _____

MITTO _____

    first person plural

        present _____

        future _____

        imperfect _____

        perfect _____

B) DECLINE THESE NOUNS.

turris   _____   senex   _____
turris   _____   senis   _____
_____   _____   _____   _____
_____   _____   _____   _____
_____   _____   _____   _____

mare   _____   incola   _____
_____   _____   _____   _____
_____   _____   _____   _____
_____   _____   _____   _____
_____   _____   _____   _____

litus   _____   delictum   _____
litoris   _____   _____   _____
_____   _____   _____   _____
_____   _____   _____   _____
_____   _____   _____   _____

serpens   _____   reus   _____
serpentis   _____   _____   _____
_____   _____   _____   _____
_____   _____   _____   _____

C) TRANSLATE THESE SENTENCES INTO ENGLISH.

1. Fames cives provinciae tempore belli terruit. _____

_____

2. Leges patriae non erat iustae. _____

_____

3. Pater liberos trans gramen laete ducebat. _____

_____

4. Iter per montes in viis asperis mulieri non placuit. _____

_____

5. Reus argumentum novum iudicibus dat. _____

_____

D) TRANSLATE THESE SENTENCES INTO LATIN.

1. The flock wandered into the valley. _____

_____

2. The settlers entrusted the money to the leader._____

_____

TEST KEYS

TEST 1

A) GIVE THE ENGLISH TRANSLATION FOR THESE WORDS AND LABEL THEM ACCORDING TO WHETHER THEY ARE NOUNS (N) OR ADJECTIVES (A).

N   campus   plain, level area   A   umidus   wet

N   heros   hero   N   argentum   silver, money

N   fenestra   window

B) TRANSLATE THESE VERBS.

1. Ridebo.   I shall laugh.

2. Portas.   You carry.

3. Lucet.   It is shining.

4. Tardabis.   You will delay.

5. Amabunt.   They will love.

6. Ridebimus.   We shall laugh.

7. Portamus.   We are carrying.

8. Tardo.   I delay.

9. Lucent.   They are bright.

10. Amabit.   He will love.

C) COMPLETE EACH STATEMENT BY WRITING "NOUNS," "VERBS," OR "ADJECTIVES" IN THE BLANK.

1. *o, s, t, mus, tis* and *nt* are endings for Latin __verbs__ .

2. __Nouns__ name a person, place, or thing.

3. Most Latin __adjectives__ have three endings so they can match the noun they are describing.

4. __Verbs__ express action or state of being.

5. The endings on Latin __nouns__ tell whether it is singular or plural and what its function is in the sentence.

D) LIST FIVE DERIVATIVES AND THE LATIN WORD EACH CAME FROM.

1. _____

2. _____

3. _____

4. _____

5. _____

TEST 2

A) FILL IN THE BLANKS.

The accusative singular ending in the 1st declension is <u>am</u> .

In the 2nd declension it is <u>um</u> *and in the 3rd it is* <u>em</u> .

The accusative plural ending in the 1st declension is <u>as</u> .

In the 2nd declension it is <u>os</u> *and in the 3rd it is* <u>es</u> .

B) GIVE THE TRANSLATION AND ACCUSATIVE SINGULAR FORM OF THESE NOUNS IN LATIN.

	TRANSLATION	ACCUSATIVE SING. FORM
1. harena	<u>sand, beach</u>	<u>harenam</u>
2. astrum	<u>star, constellation</u>	<u>astrum</u>
3. lapis	<u>stone, rock</u>	<u>lapidem</u>
4. ratis	<u>raft, boat</u>	<u>ratem</u>
5. lucus	<u>grove</u>	<u>lucum</u>

C) TRANSLATE THESE. (CAREFULLY)

1. Pecunia incolam delectat. <u>Money delights the settler.</u>

2. Incolae montem explorabunt. <u>The settlers will explore the mountain.</u>

3. Avaritia est culpa. <u>Greed is a sin.</u>

4. Ventus ratem agitat. <u>The wind is driving the boat.</u>

5. Fulmen candet. <u>The lightning is glowing.</u>

6. Nauta rates convocabit. <u>The sailor will call together the boats.</u>

7. The smoke frightens the horse. <u>Fumus equum terret.</u>

8. The groves are laurel trees. <u>Luci sunt lauri.</u>

D) WHAT IS THE FUNCTION OF THESE WORDS IN THE SENTENCES ABOVE?

pecunia in #1   <u>subject</u>

montem in #2   <u>direct object</u>

avaritia in #3   <u>subject</u>

E) GIVE THE LATIN ORIGIN FOR THESE ENGLISH WORDS:

1. sylvan   <u>silva</u>

2. floriculture   <u>flos</u>

3. lapidary   <u>lapis</u>

4. convocation   <u>convoco</u>

What element is "au" the chemical symbol for? <u>gold</u>

TEST 3

A) An adjective modifies a <u>noun</u> or a <u>pronoun</u>. It can tell <u>which one,</u> <u>how many</u> or <u>what kind</u>.

A Latin adjective matches what it modifies in three ways: <u>gender</u>, <u>number</u>, and <u>case</u>.

The three genders are <u>masculine</u>, <u>feminine</u>, and <u>neuter</u>.

B) Translate these phrases into Latin, matching everything that needs to be. Use the nominative case.

1. new road   <u>via nova</u>

2. evil master   <u>dominus malus</u>

3. intelligent watchman   <u>custos acutus</u>

4. cold building   <u>aedificium gelidum</u>

5. faithful male servants   <u>famuli fidi</u>

C) Translate these sentences.

1. Caterva rauca aedificium vitat. <u>The roaring mob is avoiding the building.</u>

2. Famuli laeti gregem novum demonstrant. <u>The happy servants are pointing out the new flock.</u>

3. Frumenta flammae ferae torrent. <u>The fierce flames are burning the crops.</u>

4. The intelligent merchant will prepare the way. <u>Mercator acutus viam parabit.</u>

D) Decline the phrase *hortus quietus* on the lines below.

hortus quietus	horti quieti
horti quieti	hortorum quietorum
horto quieto	hortis quietis
hortum quietum	hortos quietos
horto quieto	hortis quietis

What is a "hortus quietus"? <u>a quiet garden</u>

TEST 4

A) GIVE THE PRINCIPAL PARTS OF THESE VERBS FROM MEMORY:

amo, <u>amare</u>, <u>amavi</u>, <u>amatum</u>

rogo, <u>rogare</u>, <u>rogavi</u>, <u>rogatum</u>

sum, <u>esse</u>, <u>fui</u>, <u>futurum</u>

Give the present stem of amo: <u>ama</u> and rogo: <u>roga</u>.

What three tenses is the present stem used for? <u>present</u>, <u>imperfect</u>, <u>future.</u>

B) TRANSLATE THESE VERBS.

1. conciliare   <u>to win over</u>

2. peccabat   <u>he was sinning</u>

3. mutabam   <u>I was changing</u>

4. conservabant   <u>they were saving</u>

C) FINISH THE CONJUGATION OF *SUM* IN THE IMPERFECT TENSE ON THE LINES AND TRANSLATE IT ON THE SIDE.

<u>I was</u>	ERAM	<u>ERAMUS</u>	<u>we were</u>
<u>you were</u>	ERAS	ERATIS	<u>you (all) were</u>
<u>he, she, or it was</u>	ERAT	ERANT	<u>they were</u>

D) DECLINE *LABOR* ON THE LINES BELOW.

labor	labores
laboris	laborum
labori	laboribus
laborem	labores
labore	laboribus

E) TRANSLATE THESE SENTENCES.

1. Navigabuntne exploratores? <u>Will the explorers sail?</u>

2. Damnabitne iudex severus latronem? <u>Will the severe judge condemn the robber.</u>

3. Virgo proelium spectat. <u>The maiden is watching the battle.</u>

4. Porta litteras. <u>Carry the letter.</u>

5. Appropinquate ad ducem. <u>Approach the general.</u>

6. The defendant was ignorant. <u>Reus erat ignarus.</u>

7. The victors were spending the winter. <u>Victores hiemabant.</u>

TEST 5

A) GIVE A SYNOPSIS OF *CANTO* IN THE 2ND PERSON SINGULAR. EXCEPT FOR THE PRINCIPAL PARTS, INCLUDE THE ENGLISH TRANSLATION OF ALL FORMS.

CANTO <u>canto, cantare, cantavi, cantatum</u>

present	<u>cantas</u>		<u>you are singing</u>
future	<u>cantabis</u>		<u>you will sing</u>
imperfect	<u>cantabas</u>		<u>you were singing</u>

B) DECLINE THESE 3RD DECLENSION NOUNS.

vestis	<u>vestes</u>	hospes	<u>hospites</u>
<u>vestis</u>	<u>vestium</u>	<u>hospitis</u>	<u>hospitum</u>
<u>vesti</u>	<u>vestibus</u>	<u>hospiti</u>	<u>hospitibus</u>
<u>vestem</u>	<u>vestes</u>	<u>hospitem</u>	<u>hospites</u>
<u>veste</u>	<u>vestibus</u>	<u>hospite</u>	<u>hospitibus</u>

C) GIVE THE DATIVE FORMS OF THESE NOUNS.

	SINGULAR	PLURAL
1. turba	<u>turbae</u>	<u>turbis</u>
2. mater	<u>matri</u>	<u>matribus</u>
3. ludus	<u>ludo</u>	<u>ludis</u>

D) TRANSLATE THESE SENTENCES.

1. Mulier carmen gratum liberos docet. <u>The woman is teaching the grateful song to the children.</u>

2. Liberi carmina turbae cantabunt. <u>The children will sing songs for the crowd.</u>

3. Deus misericordiam populo demonstrabat. <u>God was showing mercy to the people.</u>

4. Agricola saepem bovi caro circumdat. <u>The farmer is putting a fence around the dear cow.</u>

5. The father is giving wine to the guest. <u>Pater vinum hospiti dat.</u>

TEST 6

A) FILL IN THE BLANKS.

An adjective modifies a <u>noun</u> or a <u>pronoun</u>.

An adverb modifies a <u>verb</u>, an <u>adverb</u>, or an <u>adjective</u>. It can tell <u>how</u>, <u>when</u>, <u>where</u>, or <u>to what extent</u>.

An English adverb often has <u>ly</u> on the end. To form a Latin adverb from an adjective, <u>e</u> is added to the base of the adjective. The base is found by removing the ending from the <u>feminine</u> form of the adjective.

B) IN THE FIRST BLANK WRITE THE TRANSLATION OF THE LATIN WORD. IN THE SECOND BLANK WRITE WHETHER IT IS AN ADJECTIVE OR AN ADVERB.

1. bene   <u>well</u>   <u>adverb</u>

2. praeclarus   <u>brilliant</u>   <u>adjective</u>

3. ardua   <u>steep</u>   <u>adjective</u>

4. praeclare   <u>brilliantly</u>   <u>adverb</u>

5. firmi   <u>steadfast</u>   <u>adjective</u>

C) FORM AN ADVERB FROM THESE ADJECTIVES AND THEN TRANSLATE THE ADVERB.

1. pulcher, pulchra, pulchrum   <u>pulchre</u>   <u>beautifully</u>

2. malus, mala, malum   <u>male</u>   <u>badly</u>

D) Translate these sentences.

1. Puer culmina longinqua significabat. <u>The boy was pointing out the distant peaks.</u>

2. Dux periculum civibus firme nuntiabit. <u>The leader will firmly announce the danger to the citizens.</u>

3. Avis bene cantabat sed canis male cantabat. <u>The bird was singing well but the dog was singing badly.</u>

4. Agricola canem adulescenti mandat. <u>The farmer is entrusting the dog to the young man.</u>

5. Praedones litus scopulosque vident. <u>The pirates see the shore and the cliffs.</u>

TEST 7

A) THE GENITIVE CASE IS USED TO SHOW <u>POSSESSION</u>. IT CAN BE TRANSLATED WITH THE WORD <u>OF</u> OR WITH AN <u>APOSTROPHE</u>.

Translate these words in the genitive case:

1. viri   <u>man's</u>   4. pastoris   <u>the shepherd's</u>

2. ovium   <u>the sheep's</u>   5. leonum   <u>of the lions</u>

3. mortis   <u>of death</u>

B) TRANSLATE THESE SENTENCES.

1. Vir est pastor. <u>The man is a shepherd.</u>

2. Insula erit latebra. <u>The island will be a hiding place.</u>

3. Oves sunt albae. <u>The sheep are white.</u>

4. Pastor erat asper. <u>The shepherd was rough.</u>

The last word in #1 and #2 is a <u>predicate nominative</u>.

The last word in #3 and #4 is a <u>predicate adjective</u>.

C) TRANSLATE THESE SENTENCES.

1. Vestigium leonis erat magnum. <u>The lion's footprint was large.</u>

2. Constantia pastoris gregem servat. <u>The steadfastness of the shepherd saves the flock.</u>

3. "Ego sum pastor bonus." <u>"I am the good shepherd."</u>

4. Pastor oves urgebat heri. <u>The shepherd was pressing hard the sheep</u> <u>yesterday.</u>

5. Mors ovium pastorem vexat. <u>The death of the sheep vexes the shep-</u> <u>herd.</u>

6. Oves sunt divitiae pastoris. <u>The sheep are the wealth of the shepherd.</u>

TEST 8

A) CONJUGATE *ERRO* IN THE PERFECT TENSE AND TRANSLATE IT.

<u>I wandered</u>   ERRAVI   <u>ERRAVIMUS</u>   <u>we wandered</u>
<u>you wandered</u>   <u>ERRAVISTI</u>   <u>ERRAVISTIS</u>   <u>you (all) wandered</u>
<u>he wandered</u>   <u>ERRAVIT</u>   <u>ERRAVERUNT</u>   <u>they wandered</u>

B) CROSS OUT THE INCORRECT TRANSLATION IN EACH SET.

1. postulaverunt

   ~~*they were demanding*~~   *they did demand*   *they have demanded*

2. erravisti

   you have wandered   ~~*you will have wandered*~~   *you wandered*

C) GIVE THE SYNOPSIS AS PRESCRIBED.

STO <u>sto, stare, steti, staturum</u>

    first person plural

        present <u>stamus</u>

        future <u>stabimus</u>

        imperfect <u>stabamus</u>

        perfect <u>stetimus</u>

D) TRANSLATE THESE SENTENCES.

1. Leo in urbem erravit. <u>The lion wandered into the city.</u>

2. Limen tecti est parvum. <u>The doorway of the dwelling is small.</u>

3. Legionem primam viri accusaverunt. <u>The men accused the first legion.</u>

4. The small fleet wandered through the islands. <u>Classis parva per insulas erravit.</u>

What case is *tecti* in #2? <u>genitive</u>

What case, gender, and number is *legionem* in #3? <u>accusative, feminine, singular</u>

E) WRITE THREE CORRECT TRANSLATIONS FOR THIS VERB.

accusavit <u>he accused, he did accuse, he has accused</u>

F) TRANSLATE "QUINTILI VARE, LEGIONES REDDE." <u>QUINTILIUS VARUS, GIVE BACK MY LEGIONS.</u>

Who said it? <u>Caesar Augustus</u>

Why? <u>Quintilius Varus had lost three legions in battle with German tribes.</u>

TEST 9

A) CONJUGATE *DUCO* IN THE PRESENT, FUTURE, IMPERFECT, AND PERFECT.

PRESENT

duco	ducimus		
ducis	ducitis		
ducit	ducunt		

FUTURE

ducam	ducemus
duces	ducetis
ducet	ducent

IMPERFECT

ducebam	ducebamus
ducebas	ducebatis
ducebat	ducebant

PERFECT

duxi	duximus
duxisti	duxistis
duxit	duxerunt

B) TRANSLATE THESE PHRASES AND WORDS INTO LATIN.

1. during the night   nocte   4. at dawn   prima luce

2. into the sea   in mare   5. in the year of war   anno belli

3. in the sea   in mare   6. on the mound   in tumulo

C) TRANSLATE THESE SENTENCES.

1. Securis iuvenis lignum fregit. The young person's axe broke the timber.

2. Senex nepotes simul vocavit. The old man summoned his descendants at the same time.

3. Animal defessum trans limine iacebat. The weary animal was lying across the threshold.

4. Legionem die proelii vincemus. We will defeat the legion on the day of battle.

Final Test

A) Give synopses for these verbs as prescribed.

MANDO <u>mando, mandare, mandavi, mandatum</u>

    third person singular

        present <u>mandat</u>

        future <u>mandabit</u>

        imperfect <u>mandabat</u>

        perfect <u>mandavit</u>

URGEO <u>urgeo, urgere, ursi</u>

    second person plural

        present <u>urgetis</u>

        future <u>urgebitis</u>

        imperfect <u>urgebatis</u>

        perfect <u>ursistis</u>

MITO <u>mitto, mittere, misi, missum</u>

    first person plural

        present <u>mittimus</u>

        future <u>mittemus</u>

        imperfect <u>mittebamus</u>

        perfect <u>misimus</u>

B) DECLINE THESE NOUNS.

turris	turres	senex	senes
turris	turrium	senis	senum
turri	turribus	seni	senibus
turrem	turres	senem	senes
turre	turribus	sene	senibus

mare	maria	incola	incolae
maris	marium	incolae	incolarum
mari	maribus	incolae	incolis
mare	maria	incolam	incolas
mari	maribus	incola	incolis

litus	litora	delictum	delicta
litoris	litorum	delicti	delictorum
litori	litoribus	delicto	delictis
litus	litora	delictum	delicta
litore	litoribus	delicto	delictis

serpens	serpentes	reus	rei
serpentis	serpentium	rei	reorum
serpenti	serpentibus	reo	reis
serpentem	serpentes	reum	reos
serpente	serpentibus	reo	reis

C) TRANSLATE THESE SENTENCES INTO ENGLISH.

1. Fames cives provinciae tempore belli terruit. Famine frightened the citizens of the province in the time of the war.

2. Leges patriae non erat iustae. The laws of the native land were not just.

3. Pater liberos trans gramen laete ducebat. <u>The father was happily leading the children across the grass.</u>

4. Iter per montes in viis asperis mulieri non placuit. <u>The journey through the mountains on rough roads did not please the woman.</u>

5. Reus argumentum novum iudicibus dat. <u>The defendant is giving new evidence to the jurors.</u>

D) Translate these sentences into Latin.

1. The flock wandered into the valley. <u>Grex in vallem erravit.</u>

2. The settlers entrusted the money to the leader. <u>Incolae pecuniam duci mandaverunt.</u>